WEST MEETS EAST

WEST MEETS EAST

Americans Adopt Chinese Children

RICHARD TESSLER,
GAIL GAMACHE,
AND LIMING LIU

BERGIN & GARVEY
Westport, Connecticut • London

Library of Congress Cataloging-in-Publication Data

Tessler, Richard C.
   West meets East : Americans adopt Chinese children / Richard
Tessler, Gail Gamache, and Liming Liu.
     p. cm.
   Includes bibliographical references and index.
   ISBN 0–89789–657–2 (alk. paper).—ISBN 0–89789–658–0 (pbk. :
alk. paper)
     1. Intercountry adoption—China.   2. Interracial adoption—China.
3. Intercountry adoption—United States.   4. Interracial adoption—
United States.   5. Chinese American children—Family relationships.
6. Family life surveys—United States.   I. Gamache, Gail, 1938– .
II. Liu, Liming, 1954– . III. Title.
  HV875.58.C6T47   1999
  362.73′6′08951073—dc21   98–44536

British Library Cataloguing in Publication Data is available.

Library of Congress Catalog Card Number: 98–44536
ISBN: 0–89789–657–2
    0–89789–658–0 (pbk.)

First published in 1999

Bergin & Garvey, 88 Post Road West, Westport, CT 06881
An imprint of Greenwood Publishing Group, Inc.
www.greenwood.com

Printed in the United States of America

∞™

The paper used in this book complies with the
Permanent Paper Standard issued by the National
Information Standards Organization (Z39.48–1984).

10 9 8 7 6 5 4 3 2 1

*To every child in the United States who is
American and something else*

CONTENTS

PREFACE

This book was conceived as an opportunity to document some of the issues confronting Americans who adopted children from the People's Republic of China in the 1990s. The main edifice for the book is a survey of 526 parents with children from China that was conducted in 1996. In writing the chapters, we drew on many other sources as well, including first-person stories, relevant historical accounts, and an unusual key informant perspective on Chinese culture and values. The product is intensely personal at the same time that it is social and political.

Although there has not been systematic research, there is every indication from parental reports that children adopted from China are doing very well. This contrasts strongly with portraits of some other international adoptions of traumatized and neglected orphans in countries other than China. The parents in our survey wrote enthusiastically about their children with the excitement that is characteristic of new parents everywhere. In the words of one new father, "This adoption is the best thing that has ever happened to me." But our knowledge is incomplete, as it is based much more on parents' expectations and early experiences than on outcomes rooted in middle childhood, adolescence, and adulthood.

The more than ten thousand Chinese children who were adopted by Americans between 1989 and 1997 are immigrants, albeit very advantaged ones. These children left their birth country behind, and with it their heritage, to be raised with Western world views and language at the same time that their appearance will forever mark them as Eastern. What are the implications of this dichotomy for the children, their parents, and for the evolution of American society more generally? In this book, we explore both the challenges and opportunities inherent in the dichotomy between West and East from the perspective of Americans who have children adopted from the People's Republic of China.

In this book we coin a new term to describe these families. We call them "American & Chinese families" to distinguish them from traditional "Chinese-American families" in which the ancestors of one or both of the parents emigrated from China, and from "American and Chinese" families that are formed through ethnic intermarriage. Thus we consciously break with standard grammatical usage in a way that reflects how these bi-cultural families have also chosen a break with tradition. The "&" is used to represent the intimate connection between these non-Chinese-American parents and their Chinese babies.

In raising their Chinese-born children in America, some parents choose to emphasize American culture and identity, others put an emphasis on Chinese socialization, and still others try to expose their children simultaneously to both Chinese and American cultures. These different paths are also mirrored in the backgrounds and views of the three authors. Liming Liu was born and raised in the People's Republic of China and has a strong commitment to Chinese language, culture, and values.

Gail Gamache, whose ancestors came to the United States from Scotland, Ireland, and French-speaking Canada during the great wave of immigration in the nineteenth century, believes that children adopted from China should be raised to appreciate their heritage while thinking (like other immigrants before them) of themselves first and foremost as Americans. Richard Tessler, who has two daughters from China, has a strong commitment to integrating Chinese experiences into everyday American life based on the belief that children can benefit psychologically and pragmatically from bi-cultural socialization.

Like the families under study, there is disagreement among the authors about exactly what it means to be an American and how much ethnic Chinese socialization is appropriate and possible. In our informal exchanges, Gail Gamache would typically emphasize the importance of the children feeling accepted as Americans and the need for adoptive parents to advocate for the inclusion of all ethnicities as "real" Americans. By contrast, Liming Liu tended to emphasize the benefits of Chinese socialization to prevent estrangement from a heritage that is reinforced daily by physical appearance. Richard Tessler, who of the three comes closest to a Chinese & American perspective, tended to emphasize the need to help the children to find a secure footing in both cultures.

Socializing a child in America to be competent in Chinese language, culture, and values is a formidable task for many American adoptive parents who, unlike Chinese immigrant families, do not possess "insider" knowledge to hand down to their children. Thus, it would be a mistake to infer that a majority of these children will be truly bi-cultural. Full bi-cultural socialization would require more family foundation in Chinese culture than most adoptive parents realistically can have available to them or would want to provide.

Nor is bi-cultural socialization the only issue at stake for families with children adopted from China. In looking to the future, there are several other issues that parents and their children are likely to face, including the need to explain the socio-political context that leads Chinese girls to be available for adoption, the implications of the age gap for the parent-child relationship, and the challenges ahead for Families with Children from China (FCC) as a movement committed to keeping children adopted from China in touch with their birth culture. How American society supports and reacts to these Chinese & American families in the twenty-first century will tell us much about our nation and its commitment to diversity.

We are grateful to many people who contributed in various ways to the writing of this book. Weihang Chen encouraged the first author to undertake this project by persuading him that, similar to the adoptions themselves, research about the parents and their children could serve a humanitarian purpose. Helen Snyder Cooper encouraged the first author to write down his memories of the first adoption trip while they were still vivid. Merry Cushing and Jesse Gordon helped us to design a homepage on the Internet. Zhongwei Shen prepared the calligraphy that appeared on our study web page. Dee Weber gave generously of her time as database manager of our research institute. Susan Caughman and the board of directors of FCC–New York agreed to announce the project on their Internet site. Kay Johnson had valuable input into the development of the questionnaire. Karen Mason advised us on how to conduct the mailings efficiently. FCC newsletter editors from all over the United States published the invitation to participate in the study for adoptive parents who were not reached by the Internet. Susan Avery and Maureen Corcoran made special efforts to help us reach other eligible family members through direct mailings.

While the manuscript was in preparation, the authors received valuable feedback in reaction to public presentations at the Social and Demographic Research Institute, the Institute for Asian American Studies, and the New England Chapter of

Families with Children from China. Alison Donta provided valuable information on expected population changes during the twenty-first century. Patricia Gorman, John Harney, and Deborah McCurdy reviewed parts of the manuscript in draft form, and each gave us very helpful suggestions. We also acknowledge ideas received from research colleagues around the country, especially Howard Altstein, Tom Bayh, Lisa Chen, and Victor Groza, who communicated with us while we were working on the manuscript, and whose observations found expression in the book in one form or another.

The survey was supported in part by a fellowship from the Institute for Asian American Studies of Boston, Massachusetts, by a Faculty Research Grant from the University of Massachusetts in Amherst, and by much contributed time from the authors. The actual writing of the book was supported by a small grant from the American Sociological Association's Fund for the Advancement of the Discipline. The authors take responsibility for the final product.

We want to extend a personal thank you to the 526 parents who participated in the survey and who shared their attitudes and experiences about bi-cultural socialization. This is really your book. We hope that when your children get older they will appreciate your efforts whatever your approach to bi-cultural socialization may have been.

Finally, we want to publically thank our own family members, our spouses—Hugh Gamache, Patricia Gorman, and Baitao Wang, our children—Gail Fisher, Melissa Gamache, Timothy Gamache, Carol Gamache-Taylor, Catherine Regish, Hannah Tessler, Zoe Tessler, Shiliu Wang, and Xiaoyu Wang, and our grandchildren—Christopher Fisher, Heather Taylor, Anthony Gamache, Lindsay Regish, Benjamin Gamache, Michael Regish, Constance Bosinger, and Lauren Gamache. There is an element of each of you in this book, and in this sense you are our coauthors.

We hope our readers enjoy the book and the intellectual struggles that went into it. When we could not resolve our own differences, we took solace in the observation that a strength of America is its ability to encompass different voices, and when necessary to agree to disagree. Because outcome studies have yet to be conducted, there exists no gold standard against which parental attitudes or practices can be assessed. At this point, the debate is far more theoretical than it is empirical, but the stakes involved are more than academic.

The decisions parents make in their everyday life about resolving the dichotomy between West and East will shape their children's social identities, set examples for others, and in these ways contribute (or fail to contribute) to the making of an America that is inclusive of all children at the same time that it respects cultural differences. It is in this spirit that our book is dedicated to every child in the United States who is American and something else.

Chapter 1

INTRODUCTION

Who are the new families that are appearing on city streets, in suburban malls, at Chinese Dragon Boat races, and at Fourth of July celebrations? The parents, in their forties and fifties, are obviously Caucasian, and their very young daughters are obviously Chinese. This is a book about these new "American & Chinese" families which are formed through the mechanism of international adoption.

In referring to these families as American & Chinese, we are seeking to highlight the sense in which this is a new ethnic family form, distinct from traditional Chinese-American families. The story that lies ahead is intensely personal at the same time that it is also social and political. It is a story about the making of individual families through international adoption, of the building of cultural bridges between the United States and the People's Republic of China (PRC), and of the need to change public attitudes so that persons of Chinese ancestry are recognized as full Americans. Our focus is on families whose personal biographies intersect with social history (Mills, 1959).

These families are calling attention to unexamined assumptions about what it means to be American. In seeking to have their children accepted in an America that largely excludes Asian culture from its traditions, adoptive parents are resisting the traditional dichotomy between the West and the East. In many ways, their activities fit the sociological definition of a social movement as "a large number of people who have joined together to bring about or resist some social or cultural change" (Robertson, 1981). Thus, what started as a most personal decision to adopt a child from China has fostered the birth and growth of a social movement emphasizing global rather than parochial thinking in which some adoptive parents consciously attempt to build a cultural bridge between the United States and China.

At the societal level, the visible nature of these adoptions confronts these mostly white American parents with the need to explain the nature of their becoming a family and their children's status in America. What appears at first to be a matter of children's individual identities and self-esteem is also a matter of changing American attitudes and practices. Thus, this is not just a book about Chinese children "becoming American"; it is also a book about inviting America to live up to its ideal as a nation of immigrants.

The efforts of Caucasian parents to make American society more inclusive of Chinese-Americans on the playground, in the school, and in the workplace, arise out of particular social and historical circumstances. These include a cohort of adoptive parents who came of age in the 1960s and saw the power of social activism in responding to racism and militarism, a changing relationship between the United States and the PRC, and the emergence of a global economy. Many of the parents currently adopting from China discovered in the 1960s that the status quo need not be accepted but could be changed. Thus, when their international adoptions raised questions about whether it is possible or desirable for children who come from different racial and ethnic backgrounds to be accepted as Americans without reference to their racial-ethnic origins, or whether it is possible or desirable to attempt to preserve elements of their birth cultures through bi-cultural child socialization, parents opted for change and formed groups.

At the personal level, a central concern of these adoptive families is cultural. Unlike domestic adoptions where children's questions are typically associated with curiosity about "my real mother and father," parents who adopt from China will be unable to satisfy their children's desire for personal biography, but many attempt to provide a cultural biography. Many of these parents find support in this cultural quest by joining together with other families with children from China.

Although all adoptive parents would agree that there is a need to have their children's heritage fully accepted and valued, not all would agree that there is a need to provide Chinese socialization. In fact, parents begin with different approaches. Although many parents are encouraging a high level of knowledge about Chinese traditions, language, and values, other parents settle for a relative balance, hoping to produce a minimal bi-cultural competence that allows their children to feel comfortable with both their American and Chinese heritages. Still other parents, believing that developing competence in Chinese culture is not necessary for an American child, take a different approach based on the idea that the critical issue involves citizenship and not ethnicity. Finally, some parents, believing that the children will eventually make their own choices, are content to wait until the children take the lead. Common to all is the desire for the child not to feel alienated or marginal either as Chinese or as American.

BACKGROUND

Some background is necessary to understand the circumstances of the parents and children that are the subjects of the

narrative presented here. Beginning in 1989, the PRC informally allowed foreigners to adopt orphaned children on an ad
hoc basis (formal approval did not come until 1992). It is not
known why China decided to permit abandoned children (these
children are considered to be orphans in China) to be adopted
by foreigners (Riley, 1997). One theory is that increasing contact with the outside world, as a result of China's Open Door
Policy, created a climate in which international adoptions were a
humanitarian response to China's "one child per family policy"
(Soled, 1995). Riley suggests that "foreign adoption [was] a
practical solution to the numbers of girls abandoned across the
country in numbers that were swelling the orphanages" (Riley,
1997). By the federal fiscal year ending October 31, 1995,
adoptions of Chinese children were accounting for about 22
percent of all international adoptions into the United States and
had come to represent the single largest source of adoptions
from abroad. The United States was also the major, although
not the sole, destination of Chinese orphans. By the end of fiscal
year 1997, 10,630 Chinese children had been adopted by
American parents.

The issue of bi-cultural socialization, about which this book is
concerned, results from the connection between immigration
and international adoption. These children continue in a tradition of Chinese immigration to America, while comprising a
new segment of it. They came under circumstances that are very
different from that of other immigrants. To begin with, these
(mostly) infant and toddler girls have been abandoned by their
birth parents in response to China's one-child policy (Reist,
1995). Their lives began with abandonment, perhaps in a bus
station, park, or other public place, and, for some, with a struggle to stay alive until they reached an orphanage, and for many
children, even after that. In contrast to early first-generation
Chinese immigrants, their circumstances were immeasurably
improved as soon as they arrived in America, coming to mostly

privileged homes and to a standard of living that other immigrants have to struggle for years or generations to achieve, if ever. It was like dropping into a "honey jar" as the Chinese father of one of the authors remarked.

As babies, toddlers, and young children, they are not directly involved in the decision to emigrate, but like other groups of immigrants, they are subject to the current laws or policies of both the "pushing" and "pulling" countries. They also tend to have less painful adaptations to the extent that their socialization to their birth culture is less developed. Nonetheless, their physical characteristics make them quite visible in their new homes in America, where in contrast to most other immigrants, past and present, they are unlikely to live in a neighborhood that reflects their ethnicity. The fact that their adoptive parents are relatively affluent also means that they are less likely than past immigrants to be at risk economically.

The history of America has long been written as the story of the assimilation of immigrants and the "great melting pot" (Gordon, 1964). Child socialization was largely uni-cultural, emphasizing Anglo-conformity particularly in the public school system, and the proportion of "unhyphenated Americans" among second-generation Americans was on the rise. But since the 1960s, theories of assimilation have given way to the idea of cultural pluralism, reflecting changes in patterns of immigration. There is a growing awareness of the eclipse of white predominance based on very visible changes in the racial-ethnic composition of the school and the workplace (Jaret, 1995).

During the next century, demographers anticipate that the proportions of school-aged (five to eighteen years) children who are Caucasian will dramatically decrease (U.S. Bureau of the Census, 1993). In 2000, 78.2 percent of these children will be white; by 2050, that proportion will drop to 67.7 percent. In contrast, the proportion of Asian/Pacific Island children will increase nearly 2.5 times. In 2000, 4.8 percent of school-aged children will be Asian/Pacific Islander; this proportion will be 11.2 percent by 2050.

Compared with the children of Chinese immigrant parents, immigrant children who are adopted by American parents are less likely to have their birth cultures reinforced at home without strenuous efforts. Because their adoptive parents are in large part not Chinese, the difficulty is not with American socialization, which takes place without conscious parental effort within the context of American family life, but rather Chinese socialization. When children are adopted from countries like the People's Republic of China whose culture, language, and values are so dissimilar as to be unfamiliar, American parents must decide whether and how to retain their children's connections to their birth cultures. Those American parents who choose to provide ethnic socialization for their Chinese children face a major challenge (Ramos, 1996; Groze and Ileana, 1996).

INTERNATIONAL ADOPTION

This section focuses on the international adoption of Asian children by United States citizens. Wilken has noted that more foreign born children have been adopted by Americans than by parents from any other country since the first wave of international adoptions began in the late 1940s (1995). In the past several years, international adoptions in the U.S. have averaged between 6,500 and 10,000 per year. In response to the demand, a large number of licensed adoption agencies have come into being to facilitate these adoptions.

International adoptions are structured by the social, religious, political, and economic contexts in both the receiving and the sending countries. Many social factors influence the various national policies toward migration and immigration which control the flow of children through adoption. These include current fertility rates, the legal status of abortion and of birth control, social attitudes toward single and unwed motherhood, tolerance of mixed race families and children, and the stage of economic development. Thus, countries with readily available birth control and legal abortion, late age at marriage, social acceptance of single and unwed motherhood, and a stable economy tend to have a large demand for adoptable children. These same factors also result in fewer infants available domestically for adoption. In contrast, the nations that have a surplus of infants and young children available for adoption tend to have higher fertility rates, less-developed economies, overpopulation, little external or internal public outcry about out-placements of children, and may be experiencing military conflict or civil strife.

The donor countries that supply infants and children typically have traditional family values that do not accommodate nontraditional family formations, which may make domestic adoptions less of an option (Weil, 1984). In some cases, nations may not permit either domestic or international adoptions. Islamic law does not recognize adoptions. Some Near Eastern and South Asian countries with a strong connection between the state and religion do not recognize adoption or do not allow adoption by foreigners. For example, Kuwait has no provision for adoption in its laws, and Iraq and Qatar do not permit the adoption of nationals by foreigners. Few children in Israel are available for adoption, where both domestic and international adoptions are strongly controlled, and where adoptive parents are required to be of the same religion as the child.

Where international adoptions are permitted, the process is sometimes viewed as "the commodification of children," "marketing in children," or as the exploitation of poorer countries by richer nations (Groza, 1997). Opponents of international adoptions view the process as an economic exchange of babies for money between the first world and the third world (Tate, 1990). To take China as an example, in 1993, the *New York Times Magazine* headlined a cover story about the adoptions of several baby girls from Wuhan as "China's Market in Orphan Girls." They also subtitled the story "Unwanted and Abandoned Baby Girls Have Become the Newest Chinese Export," explicitly linking foreign trade for profit with international adoption (Porter, 1993). The implication is that Chinese baby girls are an expendable surplus and for this reason are available to Americans (and others) who can afford the price (Riley, 1997).

Ethical conflicts have also been described in terms of the best interests of the larger ethnic community versus the best interests of the child in regard to adoptions that involve transracial placements (J. F. Smith, 1996). In particular, the adoption of black or Native American children by white parents has aroused controversy. U.S. domestic transracial adoptions have been objected to since 1972 by the National Association of Black Social Workers on the grounds that to deny black children their heritage and their identification as African-Americans, as can happen when raised by white parents, is to commit a form of genocide (Silverman, 1993). Although these issues are more contested with respect to domestic U.S. transracial adoptions, there are parallel conflicts in international adoptions.

On the other hand, proponents view international and transracial adoptions as a humanitarian enterprise that results in providing homes and families to children who would otherwise languish in orphanages (Porter, 1993). Groza (1997, p. 12) has noted that the Hague Conference on Private International Law "puts intercountry adoption ahead of intracountry foster care or institutionalization as the best option for children." Even Margaret Howard, an advocate of same-race adoptions, has admitted that "the alternative to transracial adoption . . . is not inracial adoption, but non-adoption, i.e. continued institution or foster care" (quoted in Simon, 1994, p. 142). Parents widely believe that the money that they need to expend in China will be used to improve conditions in the orphanages from where they adopted their children and to provide care to those abandoned children who, for whatever reason, are less likely to be adopted (Riley, 1997).

Some but not all international adoptions are transracial. For example, when children are adopted from Romania or Russia by Caucasian parents, transethnic families may be formed, but the adoptions do not fall within the category of transracial. Transracial adoption occurs only when parents do not share the same race as their adopted child. The adoption of Chinese children by white parents is a case in point of transracial adoption. Although not the most controversial example of transracial adoption, these children are nonwhite and being raised in an America that is still coming to terms with its growing cultural diversity. The visibility of these children as "Asian" presents these adoptive parents (and their children) with challenges that other adoptive families do not need to confront.

As already noted, the history of international adoption began in the middle of the twentieth century. Not until after World War II, when returning veterans and their families for humanistic reasons were adopting children from other countries, was international (and interracial) adoption viewed as a solution to linking children who needed families with prospective parents who wanted children. Silverman noted that "nearly 3,000 Japanese children were adopted by Americans between 1948 and 1962," and that "840 Chinese children were adopted, mostly by white American families, during the same period" (1993, p.104). However, by the mid 1960s the flow of international adoptions of Japanese and Chinese children had slowed to a trickle as Japan and Taiwan were becoming stronger economically and the door to mainland China was still closed.

Orphaned children from Korea began to come to America at the end of the Korean War in 1953 and soon became a primary source of adoptable children for Americans. Much of the credit for the advent of adoptions from Korea goes to Harry Holt, an American farmer from Oregon who, with his wife Bertha, adopted eight Amerasian children, and then in 1957 founded an adoption agency dedicated to helping other families adopt from Korea. In addition to the multiracial children who were the progeny of U.S. fathers (in the military) and Korean mothers, the war produced a large population of orphaned children in need of adoption. As a reflection of this need, Miller (1971) noted that although only 715 Korean children were counted in orphanages in 1951, by 1964 the total had jumped to 11,319. The Korean children typically were flown over in groups with Korean escorts.

For a variety of reasons, the number of Korean children adopted by U.S. parents declined beginning in the 1970s. As noted above, immigration policies related to the flow of children through international adoptions are in part dependent on the lack of public outcry. Korea is a good case in point. In the 1970s, North Korea chastised South Korea for permitting its children to be made available for international adoption. Then, in 1988 during its hosting of the Olympics, the Seoul government was embarrassed by TV coverage for allegedly using its children as an export commodity.

> Humiliated before the entire world, the Korean government imposed new limits on the number of children allowed to be adopted internationally. It also made adoption a more attractive option for Korean families (for instance, by finally allowing parents to add adoptive children to the official family registry and by granting adoptive families preference when applying for public housing). As a result, the adoption numbers have plummeted dramatically since 1986, when the adoption numbers peaked at 6,275. In 1989, 3,544 adoptees entered the U.S., in 1991, only 1,818, and in 1996, 1,516. (T. Hong, 1997, p. 35)

Given the large number of Korean adoptions, and the number of years involved, it is not surprising to find research about the outcomes of these Korean adoptions. One of the largest studies was undertaken by Dong Soo Kim who studied adolescent outcomes in children adopted from Korea. Kim's sample was identified through Holt's International Children's Services, which had arranged the greatest number of Korean adoptions. He compared two groups of Korean adoptees: One group was adopted before twelve months of age; a second was adopted after six years of age.

Kim found that the children adopted in their infancy, and who had been in their adoptive homes longer, had better self-esteem and tended to adjust better than those children who were adopted when they were older and who had been in their adoptive homes for fewer years when they reached adolescence. Although as adolescents children in the "early adoption" group were achieving academically on a par with their nonadopted peers, the children in the "later adoption" group were behind their age peers by a grade or two on average. However, both the early and later adopted children expressed a high level of satisfaction with their lives, and their adoptive parents were similarly satisfied (Kim, 1977).

In terms of parents' attitudes toward bi-cultural socialization, the international and social circumstances of the adoptions of children from Korea differ in some important ways from the current adoptions of children from China. First, the adoptive parents were not required to travel to Korea. Since they did not see their children's birth country, parents were unlikely to develop a personal interest in Korean culture or to appreciate the cultural losses that their children experienced. Second, the children were available for adoption initially as a result of a military conflict in which the United States was involved. Ethnic animosities tend to linger on after a conflict, and parents may have hesitated to encourage Korean culture in the face of community disinterest or dislike. Regardless, "most of the Korean children largely thought of themselves as Americans and reflected little of Korean culture in their daily lives" (quoted in Silverman, 1993, p. 108). Interviews with adult adoptees confirm this uni-cultural approach:

> For many Korean adoptees who are now adults in their 20's, 30's and 40's, assimilation was the only way of life. Some were forbidden to speak their native tongue while they were growing up. Others were simply not provided with resources for learning about their ethnic roots or culture; such resources were often not available. (T. Hong, 1997, pp. 36, 38)

It is easy to imagine how these young adults, who as children were adopted from another culture, might feel estranged from their roots. But the 1960s and 1970s were different times. In the 1990s, general attitudes about parenting children adopted internationally have changed to include some degree of bi-cultural socialization as a goal, based on the assumption that knowledge and pride in one's birth culture will serve as a defense against intolerance and racism, as a source of self-esteem, and as a replacement for individual biography.

The impact of going to China and adopting a child in cultural context should not be underestimated. Adoptive parents could be seen as "adopting from" Korea wheras adoptive parents can be said to "adopt in" China. Going to China to meet one's child is seen by many of these adopting parents as an exciting journey as it is their first view of a culture so different from their own. Finally, the availability of Chinese children for adoption is not associated with a U.S. military action, and in fact is occurring in an era of mostly friendly relations between the two countries.

The Chinese adoption experiences are also occurring at a time when the population of America is changing in terms of racial and ethnic diversity, and more interest is being shown in "roots" and cultural identity. In the 1990s, Americans are more likely than ever before to recognize the value of multiculturalism. The celebration of differences provides a philosophical basis for choosing to help one's child stay culturally connected to China. Although international adoption provides one useful perspective, it is not the only way to look at the formation of American & Chinese families. The next section takes an immigration perspective. Chinese people have their own history in America, and these children follow in a long path of other Chinese immigrants to the United States. This is also an important part of their story.

CHINESE IMMIGRATION TO AMERICA

The Chinese children who come to America through adoption are immigrants. Although the reasons for their emigration are very different from those of other Chinese immigrants, it is possible that they will experience the same negative societal reaction that other immigrants have faced. Below, we present a brief history of Chinese immigration to America because, as Schaefer has stated, "the resentment of Chinese immigrants . . . is not a relic of a century ago. Intolerance is as continuous as has been the flow of immigration itself" (1995, p. 90).

Chinese immigration to the United States was relatively unknown prior to the middle part of the nineteenth century. By 1850, there had been only forty-six Chinese people who had emigrated to the United States. But war, drought, and overcrowding in China, as well as the lure of the discovery of gold and the advent of the railroad in the western United States, led many Chinese to come in search of "old gold mountain," which is the Chinese name for San Francisco (L. H. Huang, 1976). Thus, the first great wave of Chinese immigration to the United States began during the Gold Rush and continued as American capitalists recruited laborers in China. Most of these early immigrants were not seeking permanent homes, but rather hoped to return to China after they had earned their fortunes.

To improve their lives, the early Chinese immigrants accepted the considerable risks associated with nineteenth-century oceanic voyages which could take up to two months. By 1880, more than two hundred thousand people had left China for the United States. The harsh reality of their new lives came to be symbolized by construction of the railroads, where many worked as "coolies," performing the hard physical labor of building the western Pacific railroads. The term "coolie," which is a Chinese word referring to those who do backbreaking labor, was used pejoratively by Americans. Although the predominant labor force for the Union Pacific Railroad was Irish, as many as 90 percent of the people who were hired to work on the Central Pacific Railroad were Chinese (Schaefer, 1995).

Paul Yee, a third-generation Chinese-Canadian, noted historian and author of books for children, has created a fictional account that brings to life the experiences of early Chinese immigrants working on the railroad in "the new world." Below we quote from a passage about an early Chinese immigrant named Young Chu from Yee's book *Tales from Gold Mountain*.

> Finally he arrived in a busy port city. . . . Young Chu was soon penniless. But he was young and strong and he feared neither danger nor hard labor. He joined a work gang of thirty Chinese, and a steamer ferried them up a river canyon to build the railway. . . . The crew pitched their tents and began to work. They hacked at hills with handscoops and shovels to level a pathway for the train. Their hammers and chisels chipped boulders into gravel and fill. Their dynamite and drills thrust tunnels deep into the mountain. At

night, the crew would sit around the campfire chew-
ing tobacco, playing cards and talking. [Conversa-
tions would take place about the new world.] The
white boss treats us like mules and dogs! They need a
railway to tie this nation together, but they can't afford to pay decent wages. What kind of country is
this? (Yee, 1989, pp. 11–12)

Although American capitalists welcomed Chinese men as laborers, American workers resented their willingness to work for
low wages, as well as the competition for jobs that the Chinese
represented. This resentment was implied by the use of the term
"coolie." Thus, these Chinese men came into conflict with racism and Caucasian labor unions who resented their use as strike
breakers. In addition to excluding Chinese laborers from membership, unions also did not welcome their association into their
own ethnic Chinese labor unions.

As is true with each succeeding wave of ethnic immigration,
native-born Americans tended to resent the newcomers rather
than their exploiters (Schaefer, 1995). Although whites had refused the backbreaking labor involved in laying tracks over the
rugged western terrain, they managed to prevent the Chinese laborers from being at the ceremony when a golden spike joined
the Union Pacific and Central Pacific railroads in 1869. As the
Chinese immigrants came in ever-increasing numbers in search
of "old gold mountain," an anti-Chinese movement arose
which was marked both by new legislation restricting the rights
of the Chinese and less formally by mob violence, vigilante
groups, and other forms of intimidation.

Ironically, in a nation founded by people who were not native
born, U.S. history is replete with examples of fear of foreigners
(xenophobia) and the belief that the interests of native-born
Americans should be superior to the claims of the foreign born
(nativism). The anti-Chinese movement was no exception.

Xenophobia and nativism were used to garner support for legislation and policies designed to prevent uncontrolled immigration, including laws that excluded the Chinese as a category of people entitled to immigrate to the United States.

Long before Chinese laborers were recruited to work on the railroads, an image of Chinese people as foreign and sinister was brought back to America by traders, missionaries, and diplomats. Sinophobia, which refers to a fear of anything Chinese, provided a foundation for racist theories and was grist for arguing that the economic gain from permitting Chinese immigration was outweighed by the negative consequences of contact with an alien race. More and more Chinese laborers were unwelcome in America.

In 1882, the Chinese Exclusion Act stopped legal immigration from China for ten years (in 1892, there began a series of extensions). This act not only made Chinese immigration illegal but also denied citizenship to Chinese people who were already living in the United States. In addition, it disallowed the Chinese laborers already in America from bringing their wives to join them. In 1903, the population in Boston's Chinatown included only fifteen women compared with about eight hundred men. Racist politicians continued to defend exclusionary policies by alleging that Chinese and other Asian laborers were to blame for the industrial depression of 1883–1886, that they were a source of contagious diseases, and that they were clannish and would not assimilate. Some fifteen years after the Exclusion Act, American boats patrolled the coasts to ensure that no persons of Chinese or other Asian heritage entered the country.

Persons of Chinese descent were not alone in being discriminated against according to their national origins. Chinese-Americans share the history of many hyphenated ethnic Americans, such as Greek-Americans and Italian-Americans, in having their desires to come to America thwarted by a quota restriction associated with the National Origins System which began in

1921. Contrary to the promise of America's Statue of Liberty to accept "the tired, the poor, the huddled masses yearning to breathe free," this system actually offered a welcome only to northern Europeans (some 70 percent of the openings were limited to Great Britain, Ireland, and Germany). Persons wishing to immigrate from other non-western hemisphere countries were forced to confront quotas restricting their entry into the United States. Thus, for example, the yearly quota for immigration from Italy was only 6,000 even though some 200,000 people desired to emigrate, and the quota for Greece was 305 even though some 100,000 people wanted to emigrate to the United States. Ironically, Britain's quota of 65,000 immigrants went largely unmet due to a lack of British interest in emigration (Schaefer, 1995).

Indeed, some Chinese immigrants had their own view of the Statue of Liberty. Words from one Chinese man who was asked to contribute to the campaign to collect money to build a pedestal for the Statue of Liberty have come down to us through history. In response to the campaign, Saum Song Bo wrote:

> [T]he word liberty makes me think of the fact that this country is the land of liberty for men of all nations except the Chinese. I consider it as an insult to us Chinese to call on us to contribute toward building in this land a pedestal for a statue of Liberty. That statue represents Liberty holding a torch which lights the passage of those of all nations who come into this country. But are the Chinese allowed to come? As for the Chinese who are here, are they allowed to go about everywhere free from the insults, abuse, assaults, wrongs and injuries from which men of other nationalities are free? . . . By the law of this nation, he, being a Chinaman, cannot become a citizen. (Quoted in Perea, 1997, p. 53)

Nonetheless, most Chinese immigrants were not alienated to the point of returning to China. Instead, they chose to become Chinese-Americans. Like many other groups, Chinese persons in America looked out for one another and built ethnic enclaves that came to be known as Chinatowns where Chinese culture, language, and values flourished. The activities of immigrant groups are usually a mixture of both the positive and the negative, and the history of the early Chinese-American communities is no exception. Their history not only includes images of San Francisco's Mandarin Theater, but also "tong" wars and liquor and narcotic smuggling. All of this was occurring without a significant relaxation of the exclusionist immigration policies.

We see in this brief narrative of early Chinese immigrants in America the history of their struggles to reach America, to find work and housing, to be accepted, to retain their cultures, and in so doing to fulfill their own version of the "American dream." In spite of the Exclusion Law, anti-Chinese sentiment from nativists, and maltreatment from racists, Chinese-American communities not only survived but flourished.

It was not until after World War II that restrictions against nonwestern immigration were relaxed. At this time, U.S. veterans were permitted to bring in their foreign-born wives regardless of existing quotas, and refugees from the war-torn countries of western Europe also did not have to qualify for immigration under the quota system. However, new Chinese immigration did not immediately respond to the relaxation of U.S. immigration policy. Both Taiwan and mainland China had their own policies designed to prevent emigration.

National origin as a basis for determining quotas was finally abandoned in 1965 with the passage of the Immigration and Naturalization Act by the U.S. Congress which was signed by President Lyndon Johnson at the foot of the Statue of Liberty. Passage of this act increased not only the numbers of people who immigrated but the countries where they could emigrate from. The 1970s witnessed the next great influx of Chinese coming to America from Taiwan, Hong Kong, and other Southeast Asian countries. Then in the early 1980s, the Open Door Policy in the PRC made it possible for Chinese mainlanders to emigrate, and many of them chose America as their destination. In 1985, "the Emigration and Immigration Law was adopted in the PRC which guaranteed the rights of China's citizens to travel outside China and allowed those who wished to leave the country for private reasons to do so" (Skeldon, 1996, p 441)

According to Skeldon, some 57,761 people from China entered the United States during fiscal years 1992 to 1993 alone compared with just under 80,000 for the five-year period 1982 to 1987 (1996). This also included the coming of Chinese students to the United States for training and postgraduate education. In 1978, there were only twenty-eight Chinese students from the PRC in American universities, but by the early 1990s, most foreign students in the United States came from the PRC. Only about one fifth of these students have returned to the PRC; many who had the opportunity chose instead to become permanent residents of the United States.

In explaining the positive experience of more recent immigrants, newer sociological theories question the older model of assimilation and point to the diaspora as a more accurate description (Lie, 1995).

> The idea of diaspora—as an unending sojourn across different lands—better captures the emerging reality of transnational networks and communities than the language of immigration and assimilation. . . . In articulating transnational diaspora, it is no longer assumed that emigrants make a sharp break from their homelands. Rather, premigration networks, cultures, and capital remain salient. (p. 304)

Although the model of the diaspora may apply to many recent emigrants, it is clearly not applicable in the case of children adopted from China who arrive in the United States without network, culture, or capital. Ironically, the older theories of assimilation and the melting pot will probably better explain most adopted children's experiences.

Along with this post-1965 change in immigration patterns, the image of the Chinese-American has evolved from the laboring "coolie" to a "model minority," which sets a positive example for socially responsible and achieving behavior. Although the concept of model minority is itself a subject of debate, we see more and more examples of successful and prominent Chinese-Americans, that is, an anchor woman such as Connie Chung, a writer such as Amy Tan, and a figure skater such as Michelle Kwan. It is possible that children adopted from China will gain from these positive images. On the other hand, they may suffer if negative images predominate. Given the uncertainty of the future relations between the United States and the PRC, and the ethnic visibility of these children as Asian (many Americans cannot distinguish Chinese from Korean and other Asians), their acceptance as Americans in the future is uncertain.

BI-CULTURAL CHILD SOCIALIZATION

As we approach the next century, the United States is becoming more and more a country of diverse populations. Issues of racial and ethnic identity are coming to the forefront, and current wisdom is supporting a philosophy of cultural diversity rather than assimilation. But many questions remain about both the process and the outcomes of bi-cultural socialization for the thousands of children adopted each year internationally. The ethnic socialization of these children challenges us to think in new ways about what it will mean to be an American in the future.

"Bi-cultural socialization" may be defined as the process by which children come "to acquire the norms, attitudes, and behavior patterns of their own and another . . . ethnic group" (Rotheram and Phinney, 1987, p. 24). Bi-cultural socialization implies some degree of bi-cultural competence which allows children to feel at ease and to switch back and forth comfortably as they represent their dual heritages in their everyday lives (LaFromboise et al., 1993).

Although this book is concerned with parental attitudes and experiences, the ultimate test of different approaches to bi-cultural socialization will come for their children at school, on playgrounds, at swimming pools, or at the local mall. What will be their responses to questions and statements such as: What are you? Do you speak English? Do you speak Chinese? You're *not* really an American! You're *not* really Chinese! That can't be your father! There is now in America much more awareness of the existence of a racism that was denied in the 1950s and 1960s. One goal of bi-cultural socialization is to empower children to respond confidently and securely to racist remarks.

The ethnic socialization of young children by adoptive parents that we are concerned with here broadly has two functions. The first is to educate children to take their places in American society, and involves internalizing the social rules, formal and informal, which guide everyday American life. Thus, to be Chinese-Americans, children need to become competent in the culture in which they will live their lives. To avoid marginalization among their peers, these children need to have somewhat the same experiences as other American children, such as watching Disney movies, playing sports, and learning the Pledge of Allegiance. American socialization is also a way for these adoptive children to share their parents' heritage and culture.

In addition, because of their physical characteristics, children adopted from the PRC will be identified with a subculture that the majority in America do not share. Society will tend to respond to them in terms of an Asian master status (Rotheram and

Phinney, 1987; LaFromboise et al., 1993). Thus, the second function of ethnic socialization is to provide children with positive attitudes about their own subgroup in an America that is heterogenous with respect to race and national origins.

Adoption social workers are already beginning to address the issue of helping parents, who adopt internationally, to understand there is a "family responsibility to develop a cultural plan that will help their child build an identity as a cultural and ethnic person" (Groza, 1997, p. 4). Parents are advised that:

> [a] plan should be developed to keep the child connected to his or her culture, history, and traditions. Such a plan might include celebrating certain dates that are important in the child's country of origin, preparing foods native to that country, and ensuring access to culturally significant music and books. The exact content and plan are less important than having the family think about these issues and how they can integrate this part of the child's life into their lives as an adoptive family. (Groza, 1997, p. 5)

Bi-cultural socialization may be especially important when members of the dominant culture discriminate on the basis of nonwhite racial characteristics that are easily identifiable. When this happens, prejudicial behaviors tend to produce feelings of social marginality. This is especially likely to occur when (and if) members of the majority denigrate things that are Chinese or refuse to accept that Asian-Americans are *Americans* too (Chin, 1978; Thornton et al., 1990; Ou and McAdoo, 1993; Lehr, 1996). Without pride in their Chinese heritage, and without confidence in their American identification, parents worry that these children will be especially vulnerable to feelings of marginality.

The available theories about bi-cultural socialization are to be found in the immigration literature. How a person comes to be oriented with respect to ethnic and dominant cultural identities will be importantly influenced by their socialization experiences within the family and the larger society. For most immigrant families, the process is one in which parents encourage or discourage their children to identify with their ethnic roots.

There are several models of bi-cultural socialization and competence for immigrant parents and children that have implications for parents who adopt across cultures. Some immigrant parents encourage their children to identify almost totally with the majority culture, others with their ethnic subculture, and still others strive for a balance. LaFromboise and her colleagues suggest that American children who develop bi-cultural competence will "outperform their mono-culturally competent peers in vocational and academic endeavors" (1993, p. 268). They further suggest that the belief that one can live in both cultures "without compromising one's sense of cultural identity . . . will also enable the person to persist through periods when he or she may experience rejection from one or both of the cultures in which he or she is working to develop or maintain competence" (1993, p. 259). In the best of circumstances, these adopted children will be living examples of cultural bridges for persons who are having difficulty understanding the positive value of a multicultural society.

To become competent in the bi-cultural sense that we are discussing requires at least some commitment by adoptive parents to educate their children about their birth culture. In the case of exposure to Chinese culture, which is not readily apparent in American life, competence requires opportunities to learn about the culture and the spoken and written language, and to integrate culturally specific attitudes and behaviors into one's self-identity. As challenging as this is for parents who are recent Chinese immigrants, it requires extraordinary efforts for adoptive parents of diverse ethnicities who may desire to nurture bi-cultural competence in their Chinese children.

Even when parents have the best intentions, the fact that the opportunity structure is a limited one will make it difficult for their adopted children to reach a high level of competence in the culture of their birth country. It is unlikely that values and behaviors which are identifiably Chinese will be salient in their everyday interaction, or even prepare these children to feel at home in China. But some degree of bi-cultural competence may be needed to feel pride in their birth ethnicity and to have even a minimal repertoire for feeling comfortable both in social interactions that bring the Chinese identity to the forefront and in situations that bring the American identity to the forefront (La-Fromboise et al., 1993).

To the best of our knowledge, there exists no prior study of parental attitudes concerning the ethnic socialization of children adopted from China and societal responses to these bi-cultural families. This is an important omission within the international adoption literature because, as noted, China has become a major source for parents seeking to adopt internationally, and many of these parents are struggling with issues of bi-cultural socialization (T. Hong, 1997). While writings on Chinese child development are beginning to emerge for an English-speaking readership, they have not yet included discussions of adopted children (S. Lau, 1996).

Because these children will be exposed on a daily basis to American language, values, and culture, there is less need for parents to take extraordinary steps to accomplish the American component of bi-cultural Chinese-American competence. However, developing competence in Chinese may come at the expense of American socialization, magnify the children's differences, and increase the risk of their not being accepted by other American children. A related possibility is that the children who are receiving both Chinese and American socialization will be accepted in neither culture. It is possible, for example, that members of the Chinese-American community will not accept these children as Chinese-American, even if the children identify themselves as such, just as the members of the majority community fail to recognize them as real Americans. The most negative potential outcome of bi-cultural socialization is that children develop no strong attachment to either culture, thus feeling isolated and alone without a strong reference group.

Chapter 2

ADOPTING FROM CHINA

How do prospective American parents undertake adopting children who are living halfway across the world in the People's Republic of China (PRC)? Many readers may be unfamiliar with this route to parenthood although it is becoming a more common experience. In addition to being a poignant personal search, it is also a socially constructed process involving the bureaucracies of two dissimilar nations. For many parents, traveling to China is also their first experience with the culture of their adopted children (as it was for the first author). Thus, we begin by describing international adoption in terms of the rules and regulations as they existed in the United States in the early to mid 1990s. Next, we turn to the process of completing an adoption in the PRC, illustrated by the personal story of the first author's adoption trip in 1993. It will be evident from this chapter that the process of adopting often marks the beginning of bi-cultural socialization for the parents. At times throughout this chapter we will ask *you*, the reader, to imagine yourself going through this process.

NEW FAMILY FORMS

The uniqueness of forming an American & Chinese family through international adoption can be appreciated if you compare it with the conventional process of forming a family. First, imagine that you decide the time has come to expand your family or to create one that includes children. Like most parents, you decide that the traditional form of biological family formation is your choice. You (or your partner) become pregnant and follow the path through obstetrician or midwife. Assuming you have the appropriate health insurance, the costs of birthing your child will be minimal. Nine months later (approximately) your baby is born an American citizen and a birth certificate is issued routinely. And, Grandma says, he looks just like you!

Now imagine that for a variety of reasons the above path is the one not taken. Instead, the process of creating a new family involves a home study by a social worker, an FBI check, having the local police take your fingerprints, dealing with the Immigration and Naturalization Service (INS), foreign travel, an exchange of money (perhaps even a loan), as well as getting a child who is not a newborn, and who not only may not look like you but may not look like anybody in your entire family or in your community. You are presented with a list of typical documents that will need to be assembled into a dossier. Your head spins with such new terms as INS Form I-600 and certificate of infertility. You *must* produce a personal statement (to be read by strangers) that includes everything from information about your early childhood to your previous marriages (if any), and your religion, values, and finances. Finally, the person(s) who will decide what child you will receive and from what orphanage is a half world away.

Approximately nine to twelve months after initiating the process, you will receive a passport-sized picture in the mail of the child who will join your family. Your prospective child is already six to fifteen months old! The accompanying medical report is very brief. If you choose to accept the assignment, you hurriedly arrange for your immunizations, obtain your foreign visa, and begin packing for yourself and for the infant or toddler who will return with you. Following a transoceanic flight several weeks later, you are first introduced to your child in a foreign hotel lobby, hotel room, or formal meeting room of an orphanage, surrounded by orphanage staff and other adoptive parents. Your new daughter (or less often a son) has heard only Chinese and no English.

GETTING STARTED IN THE UNITED STATES

But let's go back to the beginning. Below we describe the typical steps from the writing of a personal statement in preparation for the "home study" to the paperwork required in adopting a child from China, showing how prospective adoptive parents work with agencies to maneuver patiently and gently between the bureaucracies of two nations. Most likely your first step will be to choose and make contact with an adoption agency. As you begin to set the process of international adoption in motion, you will receive a warning something like the following which appeared in *Report on Intercountry Adoption*:

> All of you need to understand that due to circumstances beyond the control of any agency, the possibility exists that your adoption process could be discontinued by foreign nations, government action, or judicial decrees beyond the control of the agency. You must further understand that it is necessary to advance some funds to accomplish agency objectives and that the portion of those funds already utilized very possibly cannot be recovered in the event of such discontinuance. You need also to understand that in

> spite of information to the contrary, the child, when
> received, might have some undiagnosed physical or
> mental problem or might develop such a problem at a
> later date. . . . This is by no means meant to scare you,
> but to tell you simple facts of life about intercountry
> adoptions. (International Concerns Committee for
> Children, 1992, p. 46)

For those who choose to adopt internationally, a major decision is to decide on a country and to make a rational decision
based on the characteristics of the children who are available for
adoption and the eligibility requirements for adopting. For example, some countries have mostly boys available; others have
mostly girls; and unlike China, nearly all those countries that allow intercountry adoption have related-sibling groups. Countries with children available for adoption also differ in respect to
the desired characteristics of prospective parents whom they will
permit to adopt a child. Criteria may have to do with age, marital
status, and number of years married. Requirements among
countries also differ with respect to the necessity and length of
foreign travel.

For example, in India in 1996, single women and couples
married for at least two years were eligible as long as the couples were aged under 45 and the singles were under 42. Couples could have up to two previous children and singles could
have one previous child. Divorce was not a disqualifying factor.
The children were generally escorted to the United States. By
contrast, China in 1996 preferred people over 35 years of age
and allowed single men as well as single women to adopt. Also
by way of contrast, at least one parent was required to travel,
with an anticipated stay in China of 10 days to 2 weeks. If only
one person in a marriage traveled, the traveler needed a special
power of attorney. Prospective parents wanting to adopt sibling groups or boys would find few or none available in China.

Prospective adoptive parents who choose China work with adoption agencies that specialize in international adoption. (There were rare exceptions in the early and mid 1990s when families worked with an individual who guided them through the process of adopting internationally.) These adoption agencies are licensed by their respective states, and they are required to submit to the state's oversight and periodic renewal of licenses for the purpose of quality assurance. They typically employ social workers to conduct home studies of the prospective parents, which are educational and evaluative, and are required by state law, the INS, and the country of adoption. The social worker assigned to your adoption will also follow up with your family after you return home with your new child. In addition to guiding prospective parents through the process of international adoption, these agencies have the power to decide whether an individual or couple is qualified to be a parent and to so recommend to the INS, and later to a court in their state of residence.

Often, but certainly not always, the decision to turn to an adoption agency that specializes in international placements comes after being in contact with one or more agencies that specialize in domestic adoptions in the United States. Some couples and individuals continue to pursue domestic adoptions, and others are frustrated by eligibility requirements, long waiting periods, concerns about the health of the child, and the rights of birth parents. Other parents turn straightaway to an international agency, because it is their desire or plan from the beginning to adopt a foreign-born child. For most Americans, it is difficult to imagine adopting a child from another country without consulting with professionals. Some prospective parents are drawn to these agencies precisely because they provide a clear path to adopting a child, with less of a wait than is often the case in adopting domestically, which can take years. A foreign adoption is usually completed in twelve to eighteen months.

STEP BY STEP TO ADOPTION: THE AMERICAN EXPERIENCES

The process begins with the home study which is a series of meetings between you and a social worker, both in your home and at an adoption agency licensed in your state, culminating in a home study report issued by this agency. The actual procedures associated with the home study vary from state to state. You will pay an initial agency fee. This will be the first of many checks you will write to your local agency, the INS, the Department of State, the placement agency, the Chinese consulate or embassy in America, the child's orphanage (which typically requires cash), and the American consulate in China.

Contrary to popular belief, the home study is not just an assessment of you and your circumstances by the social worker, but also an assessment by you of whether international adoption is your preferred path to parenthood. In this sense, the home study is a mutual evaluation. One agency offered the following helpful advice on the Internet:

> Remember that even though an adoption home study may seem invasive or lengthy, it is conducted in order to prepare you and help you decide whether adoption is really for you. The regulations serve to protect the best interests of the child, and to make sure he or she is placed in a loving, caring, healthy and safe environment. Once you accept this premise, it will become a lot easier to follow through with what is required of you. (Adoption Quest, 1998)

One of the first assignments prospective parents receive as part of their home study is to write a personal statement, for which they are usually given guidelines by the agency. The function of the personal statement is to encourage parents to reflect on their motives for adopting a child, on the implications of adopting transculturally and/or transracially, and when the person is married, to encourage a dialogue between the spouses about the meaning of the adoption and how it will alter their lives. Typically prospective adoptive parents are asked to write a paragraph or two in their personal statement in response to each of a series of questions. This is a difficult task. Imagine discussing yourself in the most personal of ways, remembering that this description will be read not only by social workers but also by your spouse.

Be prepared to write a description of yourself including physical appearance, skills, strengths, and interests; the type of child you prefer (e.g., age, sex, race); your reasons for applying internationally; your reflections on marriage (e.g., describe your partner and the relationship); your early life (including family background, problems, and difficult experiences); your children (if applicable); your employment (including vocational goals and proposed child-care arrangements); your home, community, and neighborhood (in terms of resources for children); your religion and values (talk about in what faith, if any, the child will be raised); your finances (describe your reserve funds or other plans for financial emergencies); your health (e.g., chronic disabling conditions or medical problems and any emotional or substance abuse problems); and your parenting skills (actual practices in guiding and disciplining children) and what you perceive to be the special rewards and problems of parenthood.

Although you may express a preference for a six-month-old healthy girl, the final decision is not under your control. If you adopt from China, it will be the China Center for Adoption Affairs located in Beijing that will choose the particular child, taking your stated preference into account. The actual process of matching parent with child in China remains unknown. It is commonly believed that, in spite of the number of documents, the Center will mainly consider your age, your health, your annual income, and any record of misdemeanors. You may also hear rumors that it was a worker in a local orphanage in China who made the final determination.

At the same time you are working on your personal statement, you will be advised to begin collecting the many required certified documents that you will need. Following the custom of adoption agencies, we will refer to the collective documentation as your *dossier*. The documents in your dossier will provide written evidence of your physical, moral, and financial ability to be a parent.

To document your physical health, you must contact your doctor and make an appointment for a physical examination and ask him or her to write a letter attesting to your good health. If applicable, you may also need a certificate of infertility. Thinking ahead to the child's health, you may need to provide documentation of the safety of your well water (if applicable).

You will need three references from persons unrelated to you, who have seen you with children and who can write on their professional letterheads about your suitability as a prospective parent. Ask them to make three copies and have them notarized. In some states, you will also need to initiate a Criminal Records Check by your state Office for Children, which will conduct a records search to see if your name appears among a known list of child abusers. Also, obtain a letter from your local police department reporting your arrest record, if any. Imagine requiring this of biological parents!

You must also obtain a letter from your employer attesting to your employment and salary, and one from your bank stating the balance in your savings account. You will probably also need to supply copies of federal tax returns for the past three years.

Next, you will be told about the important role to be played by the U.S. Immigration and Naturalization Service in your adoption. This will remind you that, from the perspective of the U.S. government, your child is going to be a Chinese immigrant, and thus you need to be involved in a protracted immigration process which will be conditional on the approvals of both the "sending" and "receiving" countries. To receive a Notice of Favorable Determination, you and your spouse (and as of 1998 all persons over eighteen years of age living in your household) need to obtain two sets of fingerprints on INS cards and the "chief breadwinner" needs to fill out Form I-600A ("Advance Processing: Immigrant Petition for Orphan—Adoption") and sign as petitioner. Both the fingerprints and the I-600A form need to be sent to the INS office in your state, along with photocopies of the following notarized documents: your birth certificates, marriage certificate, and divorce or death certificate for former spouses (if applicable). You also need to enclose a certified bank check payable to the Immigration and Naturalization Service. If your home study is already complete (most are not at this point in the process), you can also enclose a notarized copy of it; otherwise, you can mail it later.

The INS will establish a confidential file for your petition to adopt a foreign born child. An FBI check will be made of your own and your spouse's fingerprints, and the other documents, including the home study report, will be examined by the INS for authenticity and completeness. The fact that the adoption agency must be licensed by your state means that the INS will generally accept the agency's recommendation, but there is no certainty as to how long it will take before a Notice of Favorable Determination is forthcoming. The process can also be delayed if errors are found in the paperwork or if unacknowledged misdemeanors are detected in the FBI check. If a problem is uncovered, the INS will inform your adoption agency of the problem, and seek further assurances before proceeding with a favorable determination.

It is worth reminding the reader that at no point can a prospective adoptive parent be certain of where the child may come from, even with an approved home study and a Notice of Favorable Determination from the INS. As already noted, the country of choice may change the rules for adoption while you are in the middle of the process, or may declare a moratorium (as China did starting in April 1993), or may cease allowing adoptions altogether. One reason to collect multiple copies of the documents for the dossier is to make it possible, if the need arises, for the prospective parent(s) to turn to another country with children in need of parents, without having to start back at the beginning of the process. Once you are sure of the country you will be adopting from (in this case China), you need to go through a process of verifying, translating, and authenticating your adoption documents. The verification procedure will be done at the Secretary of State's Office in your state. The authentication procedure will be done at a PRC consulate or the Chinese Embassy in Washington, D.C.

Before you proceed with preparing your dossier for China, the agency doing international placements comes into the picture. This is the adoption agency that will be the link between you and the China Center for Adoption Affairs. For some parents, this will be the same agency as the local one that did their home study. But if there is no suitable placement agency near you, or none with a China program, you will need to select a placement agency in another state. This is not at all uncommon. This agency will have its own fee structure, its own bilingual representative in China, and its own rules. (For example, some agencies require that the parents must withdraw if the prospective adoptive mother becomes pregnant during the adoption process.) The placement agency helps you tailor your dossier for a particular country, and will have your documents (including your home study report) translated into Mandarin Chinese. When the dossier is translated, the placement agency will forward it to the Center for Adoption Affairs. While you wait (the length of the wait has varied greatly during the 1990s), a process takes place half a world away which will lead you to your child.

At this point, you will need to decide whether to accept the referral of a specific child. Parents are free to decline a child, for whatever reason. But typically, prospective parents who are not satisfied with their referral fear that they will face a long wait for another child if they refuse this particular child. The information provided about the child is sparse. It usually contains the above-mentioned passport-size photo of the child's face and a brief medical report in both Chinese and English showing name, height, weight, and general state of health as of about two months earlier. The birth date is also given, although in many cases there is a measure of guesswork involved. These two documents, the photo and the medical report, will play an important role in your anticipatory socialization to parenthood. Seeing the photo is a particularly moving experience for prospective adoptive parents. It is at this point that you really feel yourself approaching parenthood. It is no longer a child but *your child*. You will need to decide whether to retain or to change her Chinese name. This is one of many bi-cultural decisions that you will make for your child.

If you decide to accept the referral of this child, and so notify your referral agency (who notifies the Center for Adoption Affairs in Beijing), the next step is to apply for a visa from a Chinese consulate or embassy, permitting you to travel to China. The visa application requires temporarily relinquishing your passport and some other papers for at least three days; this can be a particularly anxious period. This is a period of great anticipation as well. You find yourself feeling and acting like a proud papa or mama-to-be. Your new role will require that you prepare in a whole variety of ways for your child's arrival. You will need to prepare your home for an older baby or toddler rather than a newborn infant. Such preparations may include baby-proofing electrical outlets, gates on stairs, providing a safe and secure place for the child to sleep, a high chair for eating, a car seat for your automobile, and much more.

PREPARING TO TRAVEL

With visa and passport in hand, you are ready to travel, but the timing of your trip will be determined by the agency that referred the child. Uncertainty with respect to the start and end dates of your trip is one of the great frustrations for prospective adoptive parents. Places of employment may be more or less sensitive to the flexibility they will allow. A related issue for couples is whether both parents should travel. China *requires* at least one parent to travel, but *encourages* couples to travel when this is possible. However, for a variety of reasons, it is not always possible for both parents to travel. In the case of the adoption of a second child from China, one parent should probably stay behind to care for the first child.

As with any foreign travel, you need to make sure that you possess a valid passport, that your immunizations are up to date, and that all required inoculations have been received.

There is still one last task before you board the airplane en route to Asia. You must pack! In a real sense, packing to go to China makes concrete the bi-cultural nature of your planned adoption. It is not just electricity that you need to convert in China, but also your ethnocentric attitudes about what it takes to make you comfortable. You will realize that your assumptions about what is necessary equipment for a child in America are not necessarily shared in China, and you may need to plan accordingly. Packing for your child is further complicated by uncertainties about her *current* height, weight, and mobility.

Since the child will literally have no belongings (the clothes children wear in the orphanage are typically institutional), you need to bring everything you will need to feed, clothe, entertain, and keep your new daughter comfortable for as long as two weeks. One packing list published on the Internet included the following kinds of necessities: enough disposable diapers and formula to last two weeks (neither are widely used in China), baby wipes and tissues, baby nail clipper, toys, bottles, a snuggly if desired (you will rarely see urban Chinese mothers carrying their children in this way), clothing that includes everyday outfits, jacket, booties, hat, socks, snowsuit (depending on the season), as well as blankets and pajamas. Also included on this packing list were a variety of medicines in the event that the child was or became ill, including children's Tylenol, ointments for diaper rash, cough and cold medicine, and an all-purpose antibiotic for respiratory conditions.

You will also need to pack for yourselves, and to be prepared for the climates you will experience, knowing that central heating and air-conditioning in China are not as common as in the United States. Please remember that you will have to carry whatever you bring!

Along with all of the above, you will also need to have a secure plan for carrying the cash with you that you will need. (With the exception of local shopping for which you will need to exchange American dollars for *Renminbi*, all other expenses are paid in American dollars.) Cash is much more commonly used in China as a medium of exchange than it is in the United States. For example, in China salaries are paid in cash, and even large consumer purchases such as a television set are paid for in cash. You will be asked to donate $3,000 in $100 bills to your child's orphanage. The money to the orphanage is considered partial payment for the care given to your child while in the orphanage or in foster care. These monies will in turn be used to care for the remaining abandoned children, including those with special needs. Additional cash payments will be required for legal costs in China. American prospective parents are unaccustomed to carrying such large amounts of money and experience it as worrisome.

In 1993, when the first author traveled to China, there were few sources of information about what to expect and how to prepare for the trip. He and his spouse traveled to Hefei, the capital of Anhui province, with a group of other parents. Only one prior group had been sent there by his agency, and this group was returning home at the same time that he was leaving. Thus, it was not possible for him to communicate with parents who had adopted from Hefei. The opportunity structure for networking and obtaining helpful information prior to traveling has changed greatly since 1993, as more parents have adopted children from China, and prospective parents can turn to organized groups of parents for advice. Some prospective parents also make effective use of the Internet in preparing themselves to travel into another culture. By now it should be clear that the process of bi-cultural socialization begins for most prospective parents long before it does for the child.

As noted above, the Chinese government requires that at least one parent travel to China to finalize the adoption. The adoption cannot be accomplished through a third party, unlike some other countries which permit their children to be escorted to the United States. Most international adoption agencies send prospective adoptive parents in groups which are facilitated in China by a bilingual representative of the agency. Groups vary greatly in size, from three or four families to more than a dozen. When it is not feasible that both parents go to China, some will bring a friend or relative.

There are now many travel routes, but in the early and mid-1990s, the typical trip involved traveling from your home state to Los Angeles, then on to Hong Kong, and from there to the home city of the child. You would travel by airplane, train, and bus, as necessary. Guangzhou in the southeastern PRC (where the U.S. Consulate is located) would be the last stop before you return to the United States with your new daughter.

ADOPTION COSTS

If you are wondering how much money you need to spend, we present here a brief synopsis of the approximate fees, beginning with expenses in the United States. You will have already spent thousands of dollars before you even purchase your airline tickets. Preadoption expenses vary from state to state and from agency to agency. This section presents approximate fees that a couple might have expected to pay in 1995.

The first checks you would have written would be to the adoption agency for doing your home study ($1,500 to $2,500 plus an application fee of $175 or so). The next fee would be paid to the INS for processing Form I-600A, which in 1995 was $140 (in 1998, the INS announced plans to increase the immigration fee for filing Form I-600A from the current $155 to $405). You also will have needed to pay for the costs of acquiring essential documents for your dossier and for having key documents notarized, verified, and authenticated ($700). In addition, there would have been a variety of miscellaneous costs, such as telephone, copying, and express mailing postage ($250). Although you have not yet traveled to China, it is likely that your second agency will require that its preadoption fees be paid in advance.

Agency fees vary depending on the services they provide. The more expensive placing agencies ($7,000) will take responsibility for preparing much of the dossier for you, provide a translator to accompany you and the other members of your group in China, and give you much information in advance of your trip about the orphanage and the baby you have been assigned. By contrast, the less expensive agencies ($3,000) will require you to do most of your own paperwork and will provide more limited translation services. These less expensive agencies see themselves more in the role of an intermediary with Chinese officials.

The more expensive agencies are likely to include the costs of translating documents into Chinese ($15 per page) and the costs of visas to enter China ($80). However, if you contract with a less expensive agency, you may find that these fees are over and above the basic charge.

Costs of airline travel will vary considerably depending on your state of residence, number of travelers, and whether you request economy or business class seating. But, in 1995, you could expect the airline cost for you and a traveling companion to be in the area of $2,500 for two round-trip tickets to China and the one-way fare for your new daughter to fly back with you. What about other expenses to be incurred in China? These include hotel expenses for two weeks for two people ($1,400), food ($700), travel within China ($500), and the following fees payable in American cash: notary and other legal fees ($200), coordination fee payable to Center for Adoption Affairs in Beijing ($400), donation to orphanage ($3,000), passport for daughter ($18), and U.S. visa for daughter payable to the U.S. Consulate in Guangzhou ($200—it has since gone up to $325).

In 1993, the first author expended approximately $7,000 in preadoption costs, an additional $3,000 for airfare including travel within China, about $2,000 in hotel and food, and almost $4,000 in fees in China. His grand total was about $16,000. This did not include minor postadoption expenses to be incurred upon returning home, such as $80 (currently $125) for a U.S. citizenship application. By 1998, the grand total is closer to $20,000.

A JOURNAL OF AN ADOPTION TRIP

In the personal narrative that follows, you will experience firsthand the international part of the adoption process. This account was written by the first author (the "I" of the story) about two weeks after returning to the United States with his new Chinese-American daughter, named Hannah. In the following account, he refers to her by her Chinese first name, Huling, and only later as Hannah. This narrative is presented in the hope that the reader will experience vicariously the emotions and sights that are part of the process.

The First Legs of the Trip

On Thursday, February 25, 1993, my spouse, Patricia, and I left our home in Amherst, Massachusetts, to go to the closest airport (located in Hartford, Connecticut) shortly after 11:00 A.M. We were driven by a friend who had spent ten months studying in China, and who would help us care for our new daughter when we returned. We talked about her experiences in China, and what we might expect. At the airport, our friend gave us a present for Huling and big hugs before we boarded our flight to Chicago en route to Los Angeles, where we would meet the other adoptive parents in our group who were to travel with us to China. The flight took off at 1:00 EST with our hopes and fears and other baggage. The long and arduous trip had begun. Our ultimate destination was a city called Hefei where my daughter-to-be awaited me. I wondered what lay ahead.

In Chicago, as we waited to board our connecting flight, Patricia and I took turns minding the carry-on-luggage, and walking (for exercise) through the airport until it was time to board the flight to California. We arrived in Los Angeles a few hours later, and with some relief located our luggage in the baggage claim area. (Recall that the baggage contained everything we would need for ourselves and our daughter!) The hotel shuttle was late in arriving, but it finally did appear and took us the full three miles to the $59-a-night hotel our adoption agency had arranged as the jumping off point for the trip. That evening we walked across the street to a Mexican restaurant, and enjoyed some spicy food and Mexican beer. We readied ourselves for the trans-Pacific flight the next day.

The next morning, Friday, February 26, I tried to make contact at breakfast with the other prospective adoptive parents but was not sure what to look for. What, after all, does a prospective adoptive parent look like? Somehow we all eventually made contact with one another by the time we boarded the airplane. The seven parents-to-be in our group came from all over the country, from Tennessee, Missouri, Massachusetts, and Colorado. We would get to know each other very well!

On Our Way to the PRC

The flight to Hong Kong left Los Angeles in the early afternoon. By chance Patricia and I were seated close to a prospective single parent, giving us the welcome opportunity to become acquainted with her, but the other members of our group were dispersed throughout this jumbo jet. Cathay Pacific, the airline we were booked on, is one of the best in the world, but when traveling in "economy," the seats are about as narrow as on U.S. domestic flights. However, there were some perks on this long trans-Pacific flight, including a footrest, a warm face cloth, and an inviting menu. There were also three feature-length movies scheduled during this fourteen-and-a-half-hour flight (the return trip would be shorter as we would have the wind at our back). Although tempted, I chose to refrain from most of the free wine and spirits because I believed they dehydrate and make jet lag worse. Although at the time it seemed that the flight over was a very long ordeal, we were to learn on the flight back that traveling with small children is the real challenge.

We arrived, at last, in Hong Kong in the early evening, by Chinese time (there is a nine-hour difference between Los Angeles and Hong Kong). Technically speaking it was still Friday. Hence our biological clocks were really confused. Patricia barely slept during the flight; I had two or three hours of fitful sleep. We were very relieved to walk off the plane and to retrieve our baggage. Our placing agency had arranged for all members of our group to stay overnight in four-star hotels. Patricia and I walked out into the waiting area for our hotel van only to see that it was just departing, and so we stood around in a surprisingly humid and warm temperature for late February, waiting for the next van to arrive. At last, the van appeared and took us into downtown Hong Kong through a sophisticated highway system. In a whole variety of ways, Hong Kong is much like many cosmopolitan European cities. We checked into the hotel and decided to take an evening walk. It felt great to move around and to be among Chinese people.

The next morning we had a large and sumptuous American-style breakfast at the hotel. Little did I know at the time that the three cups of coffee I drank would be my last for ten days (there was no coffee available for us in Hefei). I exchanged some traveler's checks for Hong Kong dollars and that morning we set out, with camcorder in hand, to do some shopping. The prices seemed high, however, and we were more interested in watching people (of all ages) doing *tai chi* in a public park. We took a lot of great video pictures, the first of our trip, and used some Hong Kong dollars to pay for lunch in a local restaurant, where I struggled with the chopsticks they gave me, before taking the hotel van back to the airport.

On arrival at the Hong Kong airport, we checked in at the ticket counter at Dragon Air and compared notes with the rest of our group, with whom we would be sharing a highly intimate experience. The Dragon Air flight would take us to Shanghai, where we would be met by our Chinese translator. But upon arrival in Shanghai, the first task was to clear Chinese customs without our translator. It took about thirty minutes for our whole group to make it through. The sense of apprehension that I always feel going through customs was compounded by the sense that I could be stopped from entering the PRC where my daughter awaited me.

When I got through customs in Shanghai, our translator was jumping up and down in the middle of a crowd, holding a sign with the name of our adoption agency. I was so relieved to set my eyes on this twenty-three-year-old Chinese woman from Beijing, who was employed by our placing agency to assist prospective adoptive parents during their visits to China. She had taken an English name. To protect her privacy I will refer to her as Lily. Lily welcomed us warmly and enthusiastically in very good English.

I do not think we could have obtained the tickets for the connecting flight to Hefei on China Eastern Airlines without Lily's help. It was complicated, and from our American perspective it appeared to require much stubbornness and perseverance on Lily's part. We were rushed, and there was much pushing and shoving (I would learn that this was normal behavior in populous China) before we had tickets in hand and luggage checked for the next part of our adventure. It was not possible to make reservations in advance, and there was only one flight per day. The alternative was to take the train from Shanghai to Hefei, a distance of only 250 miles, but a twelve-hour trip.

With Lily's help, we (and Lily) made the connecting flight to Hefei. From an American middle-class perspective, the interior condition of the airplane itself was worrisome. It was dirty. The fabric on the seats was torn. But none of this mattered very much to me. What did matter was that I would soon be in Hefei. I was very excited.

We Arrive in Huling's City

Along with many Chinese passengers, our group landed about an hour and a half later with a thud, literally. It was a bad landing. There were almost no lights at the Hefei airport, and as we walked out of the plane into the cool night air (Hefei's climate is very different from Hong Kong's), I had a strong visceral sense of being on foreign soil. But our group was warmly greeted by a number of officials who had come to meet us and would provide transportation to our hotel. Once we retrieved our baggage, we piled into two vans, one for the baggage and one for us, and set out on our trip to the hotel.

The hotel turned out to be a "joint venture" involving Japanese as well as Chinese investments. Perched atop a hill, an inviting driveway led to an impressive lobby with many uniformed hotel employees. (There seemed to be no shortage of labor in Hefei.) We checked in and took a modern, Japanese-made elevator to the eighteenth floor, where all the members of our group had rooms reserved (Lily's room was on the thirteenth floor). As the elevator opened, we were greeted by a female floor attendant. (A floor attendant was on duty twenty-four hours a day, always ready to provide cold and/or hot water.) Our room was very attractive. Our only disappointment was that the hotel room contained what Americans would call "twin beds" (we never saw a double bed in a Chinese hotel).

The following morning, Sunday, we had our first experience at having a Chinese breakfast at the hotel. It was then (and every morning) served buffet style, and replete with many dishes and tastes with which we were unfamiliar, even to one who had eaten in many Chinese restaurants in the United States. A lot of the food seemed unusual to my American expectations about what constitutes breakfast: There were vegetables, seafood, steamed rice, soups, and much more that I could not label. There was also no silverware. Eating with chopsticks was a big problem for me, but I did the best I could. It is good that we had three more such mornings to get accustomed to the breakfast menu (it did change from day to day) before we had to dine there with our daughters, which of course made it more complicated. I cannot speak for the rest of the group, but I had yet to feel at home in China.

We Are Introduced to Our Babies

The big event of this first day was that we were told we would meet our daughters in the afternoon. People from the orphanage and from the Department of Civil Affairs would bring them to the hotel lobby. We waited expectantly in our hotel rooms, and then at last Lily telephoned to say that the babies were downstairs. When we reached the lobby, it was filled with people from the orphanage, officials, caregivers, and babies. As I approached the babies, I felt anxious that I would not recognize Huling. The babies were, in fact, hard to distinguish because they were bundled up in many layers and wore hats. Later I was to understand that this is because there was no heat anywhere (well, almost anywhere) except in the hotels for foreigners, and after all it was still early March. Patricia recognized Huling first. She was in the arms of her Chinese caregiver, who stood to greet us. Patricia cried tears of joy. Huling looked coolly at us. I worried how I would bond with this little person (at nine months, she weighed under fourteen pounds, far less than most American girls weigh at the same age), and how the adoption and our life together would all turn out. I told myself to trust in the moment, and joined the entourage as they got on the elevators to go up to Lily's room on the thirteenth floor (note that, for cultural reasons, most American hotels have no such floor), where the entire group would congregate.

The chaotic scene in Lily's room was quite stressful for me. There were four babies, seven American adoptive parents, and an equal number of Chinese-speaking people, with Lily as the only bilingual presence. Through Lily, I asked the Chinese caregiver what Huling liked to do. I was told that she liked to stand, and to rub foreheads. Was that all I needed to know? I felt close to my new daughter right away, but she was obviously more comfortable in her caregiver's arms than in mine. Quite frankly, I did not have a lot of experience holding babies.

After about forty minutes, our entire group experienced our first separation from our new daughters. As I watched my daughter leave the hotel with her caregiver, I was overwhelmed by feelings of affection, as well as a growing sense of what parenthood entails. I hoped that I would see her again very soon.

We Visit the Orphanage

Adoptive parents want as many details as they can acquire about their children's life prior to the adoption. So it seemed natural that our group wanted to visit the orphanage where we believed most of our children had been living since their abandonment. In actuality, we learned that many of the children in our group had spent at least some time in foster families. In Huling's case, she had been raised by a foster family in a rural village for her first five months until she was selected for international adoption.

Responding to the interest we expressed, the Chinese officials arranged for us to visit the orphanage the following day and for our daughters to be present. A large van brought our group to a building located in an industrial area on the outskirts of Hefei. We were warmly welcomed by all the employees and the director of the orphanage, who greeted us in a large central courtyard around which this two-story building was constructed; wide walkways faced the courtyard. I spied Huling with her caregiver, who let me hold her during our tour. I was relieved that Huling seemed more comfortable this time.

We were surprised to discover on our tour of the orphanage that most of the children were boys with special needs. There were also some older girls living in the orphanage. We were allowed to take photos of the orphanage as well as to use our camcorder. On taking leave, it was once again hard for us to say good-bye to our daughters. The bonding process was beginning.

We Wait to Complete the Adoption

That same week, the Chinese officials were scheduling time with the Chinese court for legal proceedings necessary to the adoption. As I would learn, there was much involved, and later in the week we would visit the court in person for a formal interview. Not until Saturday would we receive the official documents that would make Huling ours. This would include a birth certificate, a certificate of abandonment, a certificate of adoption, and a Chinese passport.

According to Chinese law, the babies could not be given to members of our group until the process with the Chinese court was consummated. Since there was a break in the action, we decided to go "sightseeing" on Tuesday. We made an interesting day of it, beginning with a group visit to a public park, and to a department store where we bought powdered milk along with powdered rice cereal that needed to be cooked before it could be fed to the babies. I also bought audiotapes to take back to Amherst for Huling and Liming Liu's one-year-old daughter.

Throughout our sightseeing, we were constantly the center of attention. As we waited outside the department store for our van to meet us, we were approached by many curious Chinese people, some of whom had never seen Americans before. Others even knew some English and were able to engage us in friendly conversation.

At the end of the day of sightseeing, we were invited to dinner at the home of a high official. Our genial host introduced us to his wife and four-year-old daughter. As is customary for special guests, we had dumplings for dinner, and in fact we all participated in making one of the batches using chopsticks. What a bicultural experience that was! I spent much of the evening trying to stay warm, as the official's apartment was unheated. But what was lacking in material comfort was more than offset by the good humor and warmth shown to the entire group despite a considerable language barrier. I did not realize it, but this would be our last evening as a married couple without children. At the end of the evening Lily informed us that it was our host's decision that we would be given custody of the babies the following afternoon.

We Experience Bi-cultural Parenthood

On Wednesday, the Chinese brought the babies individually to our respective rooms, where we would receive final training and be responsible for twenty-four-hour care. After the caregiver provided sketchy information concerning feeding, sleeping, and clothing, it was time for her to leave Huling with us for the first time. Huling reacted to her new parents as she would to strangers. She shrieked. She cried for two hours straight. We missed dinner. Huling was disconsolate and we were nearing a similar state. Then a curious thing happened. There was an electrical outage and the lights went off throughout the hotel. The only light I had was a pen light. I inadvertently flashed it on the ceiling and Hannah stopped crying. She was fascinated. Time passed and finally she went to sleep, and so did her weary, stressed-out parents.

As new parents, we were in the midst of a big adjustment, where the adjustment to parenthood was concurrent with our adjustment to a different culture. It was intense. The initial forty-eight hours included fitful sleeping, tearful feedings, difficult dressings, and a major problem with diarrhea. We received a quick introduction to the mechanics of diapering. By Friday, we were very worried about the diarrhea, and decided to seek medical attention. Lily arranged for the people from the orphanage to drive us to a hospital-based clinic. We walked into an unheated doctor's office around 6:00 P.M. on Friday evening, where a male doctor was present to diagnose and treat Hannah. I considered myself fortunate to have access to medical care at night. On the other hand, as an American used to high-technology medical care, I was surprised to see the doctor use a regular flashlight to examine Hannah's ears and throat. However, he did accept the stool specimen I had brought in a neat package, and arranged for it to be examined in the "lab." We were assured that the problem was not serious and were given not one, not two, but three medicines for Hannah's diarrhea. The diarrhea continued until we reached home.

While present at the clinic, we came upon a girl who had been abandoned earlier that same day somewhere near the hospital. This was an older and possibly handicapped child who appeared to be around eighteen months of age but was not able to walk. It was really heartrending to see an abandonment close up, to think about Hannah's own abandonment, and to wonder what Hannah's future would have been like if she were not adopted.

The next day, Saturday, we completed the adoption formalities. The officials and staff came to our hotel room and accepted our donation to the orphanage. Patricia and I exchanged gifts with Hannah's caregiver, and then there was a ceremony commemorating the event and celebrating that we were now Hannah's parents. This experience was repeated for everyone in our travel group.

Although we were scheduled to depart from Hefei on Sunday, there was a glitch (the appointment with the U.S. Consulate in Guangzhou could not be arranged until Wednesday), and as a result, we had an extra day in Hefei. With so many families for the consulate staff to meet with, it was difficult to obtain an appointment that matched our travel schedule. As a result, our return to the United States was delayed by twenty-four hours. We used some of this extra time to take our new daughter to the "English Corner." Picture American parents with a newly adopted Chinese daughter going to a public park in China where Chinese college students go each Sunday morning to practice their English (similar events occur in other Chinese cities)! We became part of this incredible event. There were about a hundred people at the English Corner in the park when we arrived. Many were already engaged with one of the other members of our group. About thirty people surrounded Patricia, and another thirty engaged Hannah and me. I was asked questions about America and American culture for almost an hour by several of these friendly and interested Chinese students while the others listened intently. When Hannah became fussy in my arms, I explained that I needed to walk with her. The entire group walked with us around the park as we continued our dialogue.

All that remained was to obtain a visa for Hannah to enter the United States. This had to be done in Guangzhou, a major city in southern China where the U.S. Consulate is located.

The Final Leg in China

On Monday, the group prepared to leave Hefei to fly to Guangzhou some twenty-four hours later than originally scheduled. Our translator, Lily, could not accompany us. We sensed that the stay in Guangzhou would be complicated. To obtain entry visas, our children were required to have medical exams at a clinic authorized by the U.S. Consulate, and to have photographs taken that met American specifications. We accomplished all of this on Tuesday, but getting through the bureaucracy and finding our way around Guangzhou without Lily required all the resources the group could marshal. Fortunately, we were staying at a fine hotel where there were many other English speakers. The babies were also getting easier to manage. I was having lots of positive feelings toward members of the group, and was grateful for the help they gave to me and Patricia.

On Wednesday morning, each member of our group was interviewed separately by a representative of the U.S. Consulate who also reviewed our documents. The interviews were almost anticlimactic. That evening, our group had a big celebration and looked ahead to the trip home. I realized that we were all part of a cohort of parents and babies coming from the same place, and that in some ways only the group members would fully understand what we experienced. Maybe the children will get in touch with one another as they grow up. They are all Hefei babies!

The Family Comes Home

It had been only two weeks since we had left Amherst, and now we were ready to return home as parents. The van to the airport left Thursday at 8:00 A.M., and Hannah, Patricia, and I were the last to arrive. We threw our luggage aboard, and off we went for what was to be an almost thirty-hour trip home, beginning with a short flight from Guangzhou to Hong Kong (where our children could not accompany us to the baggage claim area because they did not have Hong Kong visas) and then the long flight on Cathay Pacific from Hong Kong to Los Angeles. Alas, every seat on the jumbo jet was taken, and Hannah spent all twelve hours on our laps. It was rough for all of us. Patricia and I could not eat at the same time, since one of us had to be holding the baby. Hannah's diarrhea was unrelenting and we changed many dirty diapers in the airplane bathroom. Finally we arrived in Los Angeles exhausted and glad to be on the ground.

After passing through immigration (for Hannah) and customs (for the whole family) we bade farewell to our companions of the past two weeks, and set our own course for Amherst. First we flew to Chicago, and then from there to our local airport in Hartford, Connecticut. We were delayed in Chicago due to a snowstorm, and finally arrived in Hartford shortly before midnight on March 11. Another good friend was there to meet us and drive us home. It felt strange but wonderful to be back. Patricia and I both felt proud of what we had accomplished.

The accomplishment of course was Hannah, now nine-and-a-half-months old and growing an attachment to Patricia and me, as we were to her. We were at last beginning to learn how to care competently for her, and I think she sensed this too. The house was warm when we arrived and one of Hannah's new uncles was there to greet her. We put a sleeping Hannah in her crib in her own room (how American!) and decided to call it a night, or was it a day? We had gone through Thursday twice, having crossed the international date line. The first chapter in our life as a bi-cultural family was now complete.

THE SECOND ADOPTION

Little did I know in 1993 that two years later Patricia and I would adopt a second child. She was also from Hefei, China. Xinshen joined our family in March 1995. We named her Zoe.

The process of adopting Zoe was similar in many respects to the process of adopting Hannah. We needed to repeat every single step listed above, from having a new home study done, and new letters of reference, and a new FBI check, to a new financial statement. It is an advantage of a second adoption that we already had in our file birth and marriage certificates, and previous personal statements that could simply be reworked. We also used the same local agency, were assigned the same social worker, and in general we were much less anxious about the process. This time we wanted to welcome a toddler into our family. The passport-size picture we finally received was of a beautiful Chinese girl with a delightful and mischievous twinkle in her eyes, who at the time of adoption would be seventeen months old.

Patricia and I were faced with the dilemma that parents face in second adoptions, namely, whether one or both of us would travel. In our case, I chose to stay at home to care for Hannah, and Patricia went to meet Xinshen. She traveled with a friend who shared the experience with her and helped in many ways with traveling, child care, and so on. I extended power of attorney to my spouse, which was required by China in the event that one parent did not travel.

Instead of traveling with the group to Hong Kong, Patricia and her friend chose to go first to Beijing, where they spent a full four days, and then took an overnight train to Hefei. From such experiences, Patricia gained much more of a sense of our daughters' Chinese birth heritage. She was warmly welcomed back at the Hefei orphanage by the director and staff, and was told about plans to use monies donated by adoptive parents to add a new building. (The new building has since been completed.) Just a few months after Patricia's visit, all Chinese orphanages were closed to foreign visitors. The ban is currently being relaxed.

I first met Zoe when she and her mother disembarked from the airplane in Hartford, Connecticut. She was asleep when I first held her in my arms. But after we had arrived home, around midnight, and Patricia had retired for the evening, Zoe was fully awake and ready to explore her new environment. For two hours I followed her around the house before I could coax her to go to bed. By 5:00 A.M. the whole family was awake, and the sisters were introduced. Hannah was delighted with her new sister.

With the encouragement of our Chinese friends in Amherst, Hannah would learn to call her sister "mei mei" which means "younger sister" in Chinese. Zoe, in turn, would learn to call Hannah "jie jie" which means "older sister."

THE END IS REALLY THE BEGINNING

You have come to the end of the story of how, in the early and mid 1990s, it was possible to form an American & Chinese family through international adoption. But, the journey through parenthood has just begun. Although you have left the country of China behind, there is much ahead, including America's response to your children and the decisions you will face as to whether and in what ways to encourage the development of a Chinese as well as an American identity. In the next chapter you will meet the 526 parents who participated in *The Bi-cultural Chinese-American Child Socialization Study*.

Chapter 3

THE NEW AMERICAN &
CHINESE FAMILIES

The current chapter focuses not on individual stories but on the collective experiences of a large sample of parents who adopted from China. We launched the study *Families with Children from China: A Study of Bi-cultural Child Socialization* in the spring of 1996. This chapter describes the details of this study which asked 526 adoptive parents about their experiences. The 391 Chinese-American children that you will meet in these pages are but a small proportion of the more than 10,000 Chinese children adopted between 1989 and 1997. This chapter also details the research design, including procedures for sample selection. In addition, we describe the use of the Internet as a particularly novel method for recruiting respondents, as well as more conventional avenues.

RESEARCH QUESTIONS

The research questions were communicated to participants in the following words: "The current study aims to explore how

American parents try to cope with raising a Chinese child in American society. How, if at all, do parents encourage bi-cultural socialization? What opportunities are available to them? What barriers do they encounter? What challenges do adoptive parents face in nurturing emerging identities and self-esteem in their Chinese American children?" Since most of the parents had only recently adopted, we reasoned that bi-cultural socialization was probably more of an issue of attitudes than of actual practices. Thus, the survey focused on the importance that parents attached to nurturing or reinforcing their children's connection to their birth country.

The decision by the research team to focus on bi-cultural socialization was based on our observation of an emerging belief among adoptive parents that appeared to us to represent a new trend. In the past, parents who adopted internationally did not attach much importance to socializing their children in their birth cultures. Thus, the belief that Chinese socialization would be a positive force in their children's lives seemed new. In fact, there was evidence of a genuine social movement surrounding the preference for Chinese socialization in that parents have formed organizations and joined in community activities to achieve their goals (Youtz, 1997). As researchers, we wanted to see whether the impression given by anecdotal reports could be documented empirically. How important was Chinese socialization to American parents?

The circumstances of these adoptions provide some insights into the desire to provide bi-cultural socialization. First is the fact that many adoption agencies with China programs recommend affirming the child's cultural and national heritage as an important part of being an adoptive parent. Thus, the seeds are sown from the very beginning of the adoption process. Second is the mandated travel to China. Having traveled to China themselves, these parents are more aware of the cultural loss that is incurred, and over the long term look to bi-cultural socialization as a partial way to make up for the cultural loss. Third, many parents also want to express their gratitude to China for the gifts of these children. Contrary to the view that the children are the lucky ones, the adoptive parents believe that they are "the lucky ones."

The emergence of organized groups of Families with Children from China (FCC) reflects all these factors. Some parents are initially drawn into the social movement, because they want to prevent culture shock and make the children's transition from China to America as smooth as possible. FCC provides one such avenue with its Chinese culture programs. Interaction with FCC members tends also to reinforce the already felt parental obligation to provide their children with Chinese socialization in some form. As FCC expands its membership, its resources increase, and the social movement gains momentum.

The American media may have also fueled social awareness of the issue of identity in adoptions from China. In 1996, an influential article appeared in the *Boston Globe*, which brought into focus the identity problems of a woman then in her twenties who was adopted as a young child in Taiwan by non–Asian-American parents in 1972 (Lehr, 1996). Julia Ming Gale, the subject of this article, is confused about her cultural identity, even with loving parents who had lived for a time in Taiwan, spoke Chinese, and who later introduced Chinese culture into their Seattle home. However, her parents delayed emphasizing Chinese identity until she was twelve years old. She fought her parents' efforts to revive or develop her Chinese side. Most of the time she did not want to be any more Chinese than she had to be. The imagined face she saw in the mirror had curly red hair, green eyes, and a few freckles, and was not Chinese.

In this portrait of Ms. Gale we find a young person caught between two identities, wanting to be American but not feeling accepted in a Caucasian-dominated society. In college, she tried going "all Asian," but it felt "phony," like she was putting on a show. Her struggle includes identity confusion and feelings of social marginality which continue into her early adulthood. In Ms. Gale's own words, "The thing I most resent is . . . the fact that I can't really claim the [American] culture I grew up in, because people will never really let me."

Her observations highlight the second focus of the research, that is, the societal response to families with children adopted from China, which is something that parents have less control over than whether to raise their children bi-culturally. How will these children be accepted in American society? How will they be accepted by the Chinese-American community? How much will they find themselves as well as their adopted children the targets of racism? How much support will the families receive, and from whom?

This chapter tells the story of the research, including the use of the Internet as a partial basis for recruiting study participants. It also presents a detailed sample description, discusses reasons for adopting and for choosing China, and assesses the strengths and weaknesses of the study.

SAMPLING

As the gatekeeper to America, the Immigration and Naturalization Service (INS) is the only national source of statistics on foreign adoption. Ideally, we would have liked to sample randomly from the total population of parents who adopted from China, but were told that the Privacy Act prohibits the INS from sharing information about foreign adoptions. As an alternative, we turned to FCC, a national parents' group that is in the forefront of advocating and supporting Chinese socialization. In 1996, FCC was estimated to include over three thousand families all over the United States. Their board of directors gave us permission to announce our study on their Internet page and link our survey Web site to it.

FCC

As published on the Internet,

> Families with Children from China is a network of parent support groups in the United States, Canada, and the United Kingdom. While some of the chapters . . . are formally organized organizations with bylaws and boards of directors, others are less structured groups of families who support one another with a variety of activities. Virtually all FCC chapters shared the following three goals: To support families who've adopted in China through post-adoption and Chinese culture programs; To encourage adoption from China and support waiting families; To advocate for and support children remaining in orphanages in China. FCC chapters generally organize some or all of the following activities: newsletters, membership directories, family picnics and pot-luck suppers, celebrations of Chinese festivals and holidays, pre-adoption information meetings, playgroups, Chinese language and culture classes for children, [and] parent speakers. (Caughman, 1998)

There are three guidelines for forming a local FCC chapter. The first is that adoptive parents of all religions and marital statuses be permitted to join and that the only criterion for adoptive parents is that their child be of Chinese origin. A second guideline is that the chapter not be organized or run for profit. Finally, the third guideline is that the chapter not be associated with a particular adoption agency or individual facilitator of international adoptions.

The Internet

The study Web site was designed with a home page that extended an invitation to parents who adopted a child (or children) from China to participate in a study of bi-cultural child socialization. The Internet address was http://www.umass.edu/sociol/bi-cultural. Persons who visited the Web site could click on the underlined phrases for further information. In June 1996, we went online and in the first month received well over one hundred requests for the questionnaire. Each parent was instructed to fill out the questionnaire alone; spouses and partners were encouraged to request their own questionnaire.

The Study Web Site

Potential participants were presented with the following formal invitation:

An Invitation to Participate in a Study of Bi-Cultural Child Socialization

You are cordially invited to participate in a study of adoptive parents of Chinese children from all over the United States. The purpose is to study bi-cultural child socialization focusing on the development of both American and Chinese identities. You will be in the company of up to 250 other parents, each of whom will be asked to fill out a questionnaire.

The following informational paragraph oriented viewers to the background and scope of the research:

Richard Tessler, a sociologist in the *Social and Demographic Research Institute* at the University of Massachusetts (adoptive father of *2 Chinese daughters* and member of FCC) has received a research grant from the *Institute for Asian American Studies* in Boston for *"An Exploratory Study of Chinese-American Adop-*

tions." Pending future funding, participants will have the option of being part of a longitudinal study that will look at bi-cultural child socialization over time. The *questionnaire* should take about 30 minutes to complete. All opinions are valued. Participation is totally voluntary and absolutely confidential. No individual will be identifiable in any publication or presentation. All participants will receive a report at the end of the study. You may communicate your interest in any of the following ways:

1. by e-mail (address deleted)

2. by mail (address deleted)

3. by telephone (telephone number deleted)

Three separate links identified the principal investigator, the research institute with which he is affiliated, and the institute which cosponsored the study. These are reprinted below.

Richard Tessler

RICHARD TESSLER is a Professor of Sociology and Associate Director of the Social and Demographic Research Institute at the University of Massachusetts in Amherst. He received his Ph.D. in 1972 from the University of Wisconsin, and also held a post doctoral appointment at Wisconsin. With the exception of a year at the NIMH, he has been at Massachusetts ever since. He has done research on help-seeking behavior, prepaid group practice, children's use of medical services, and community support programs for persons with serious mental illnesses. During the past 12 years he has helped to develop a line of research on the family experience of mental illness, and is currently working on a book entitled *Mental Illness in the Family: Dilemmas of Kinship*. He is a past Associate

Editor of the *Journal of Health and Social Behavior*
and is currently a research fellow of the Institute for
Asian American Studies in Boston where he is beginning a new line of research on Chinese-American
adoptions.

Social and Demographic Research Institute

The Social and Demographic Research Institute
(SADRI) has served as the research arm of the Department of Sociology at the University of Massachusetts for nearly thirty years. Its broadly defined
mission is to support the social and demographic research endeavors of affiliated faculty and researchers.
SADRI provides direct administrative, technical and
data archive support for the funded research activities
of faculty members and research assistants. Research
at SADRI covers a broad range of topics and specific
funded research projects change from one year to the
next. Among the sponsors of recent SADRI research
are the National Science Foundation, the Rockefeller
Foundation, the MacArthur Foundation, the National Institute of Mental Health, and the Environmental Protection Agency. Douglas L. Anderton is
currently Director of SADRI. Peter H. Rossi is the
Director Emeritus.

Institute for Asian-American Studies

Responding to the urgent need for information
about Asian Americans, the Institute for Asian American Studies serves as a center for research and policy
analysis. Located at the Boston Harbor campus of the
University of Massachusetts, the Institute was estab-

lished in 1993 with support from Asian American communities and direction from the Massachusetts state legislature. The Institute brings together resources and expertise within both the 5 campus University of Massachusetts system and the community to conduct research on Asian Americans; to expand Asian American studies in the curriculum; and to strengthen the community development capacity of Asian Americans.

Two Chinese Daughters

As has been emphasized, the first author is an adoptive father of two daughters from the PRC. On the Internet, this link reproduced photographs of the first author's daughters, Hannah and Zoe, including their birth dates and Chinese first names written in Chinese.

The next two links described the study and its purpose, as well as the questionnaire.

An Exploratory Study of Chinese-American Adoptions

Although adoptions by Americans of Chinese children have been ongoing for several years, research on the topic is just beginning. Most of what we know about the outcomes of Asian-American adoptions come from fragmentary reports of the Korean experiences which now date back over 20 years. A recent review of this literature concluded that these studies largely ignored multi-cultural issues for both the adopted children and their families, focusing solely on the child's identification as American. The current study aims to explore how American parents try to cope with raising a Chinese child in American society.

How, if at all, do parents encourage bi-cultural socialization? What opportunities are available to them?
What barriers do they encounter? What challenges do
adoptive parents face in nurturing emerging identities and self esteem in their Chinese American children? This research is being funded by the Institute
for Asian American Studies and a Faculty Research
Grant given to Richard Tessler by the University of
Massachusetts at Amherst.

Questionnaire

The Chinese American Adoption Questionnaire you
will be asked to fill out will consist of the following
sections: On the COVER PAGE we will ask you to fill
in your name, address, and phone number for contact
purposes only. (Your answers will be entered into a
computer by identification number only.) You will
also be asked for BACKGROUND INFORMA-
TION. This section collects basic information, including demographics, about you, your child(ren),
and other household members. THE ADOPTION
EXPERIENCE section collects basic data about your
adoption experiences and attitudes. The section entitled, ATTITUDES TOWARD CHINESE CUL-
TURE, asks about your attitudes toward many
different ways of reinforcing Chinese identity. The
section entitled, ATTITUDES TOWARD AMERI-
CAN CULTURE, asks about your attitudes toward
many different ways of reinforcing American identity.
The section entitled, SOCIAL FORCES INFLU-
ENCING BI-CULTURAL SOCIALIZATION,
asks how much social support there is for your preference in bi-cultural socialization, and also how the

larger society may be responding to your bi-cultural family.

About These Characters

Above each page were four Chinese characters. If a viewer clicked on any of these characters he or she received a translation and explanation.

Jing (4) Qing (3) Guang (1) Lin (2) are the Chinese pronunciations (ping yin) of the above four Chinese characters. The phrase means "You are cordially invited to participate," and is often used on party invitation cards. The numbers in parentheses represent the four tonations of Mandarin Chinese pronunciation.

Other Sampling Strategies

The Internet was not the only method of recruiting families. Several local chapters of FCC also announced the research in their newsletters, and FCC–New England included a flyer describing the invitation to participate in the study in a direct mailing to its over three hundred members. As the summer went on, we received proportionately more requests in response to newsletters, flyers, word of mouth, and the article in the *Boston Globe* which mentioned the study in the context of describing the identity problems of Julia Ming Gale.

Data Collection Procedures

Although all respondents filled out the same questionnaire, the procedures for recruiting the sample varied somewhat depending on the way in which respondents learned about the study. Those who enrolled through the Internet had four choices as indicated in the orienting paragraph printed above.

Most chose to respond either directly through a special RSVP Internet link or directly to Richard Tessler's e-mail address. All such communications were answered with a personal electronic message from him. A document was constructed that was electronically sent to potential respondents who enrolled over the Internet, thanking them for their interest and asking for clarification of items such as whether both parents wanted to participate and current ground mail addresses. Similar procedures were followed for those who responded through Richard Tessler's voice mail. The fewest requests were by ground mail, and these requests were taken literally, such that if a respondent said "I would like to participate . . . " we sent one questionnaire and if the letter said "We would like to participate . . . " we sent two questionnaires (in separate envelopes).

Richard Tessler received many inquiries from prospective parents, as well as from parents who had already adopted. Prospective parents were not eligible unless they brought their children home before enrollments ended on October 31. As noted above, the questionnaire was appropriate only for parents who had already completed their adoptions.

The questionnaire was a sixteen-page document. A cover letter notified parents that return of the questionnaire signified their informed consents. An enclosed Information Sheet summarized the elements necessary for an informed consent, including the title of the project; the name and address of the principal investigator; the purpose of the research; eligibility, sponsorship, procedures including duration of task, possible risks, safeguards for confidentiality; and possible benefits. A stamped, preaddressed return envelope was included with the questionnaire. A reminder postcard was sent five to six weeks later if a questionnaire had not been returned.

In general, there were very few cases of missing data. On the several occasions when evidence indicated that missing information was due to oversight and not an unwillingness to provide the information, parents were mailed replacement pages and asked to fill them out and return them. An example of the former was when two facing pages were left blank but everything else was filled out; an example of the latter was when income was left blank but everything else on the page was filled out.

Questionnaires were sent to 587 eligible parents in 373 families and completed by 526 parents (90 percent response rate) in 361 families (97 percent response rate) in 38 states. The 61 parents who did not return the questionnaire were disproportionately husbands whose wives enrolled them. Thus, in many cases, the nonresponding parent had been sent a questionnaire on the strength of their partner's suggestion and had not directly enrolled themselves. Of the 526 parents who completed the questionnaire, 38 percent learned about the study over the internet; 35 percent learned about the study through FCC newsletters and flyers; 11 percent heard about the study through word of mouth from family members, friends, neighbors, members of their travel group or play group; 13 percent heard about it from their spouse or partner; and 3 percent heard about the study in some other way such as in the newspaper or from the adoption agency or social worker. As we will report in subsequent chapters, there were relatively few significant differences between how respondents were recruited and their bi-cultural attitudes and experiences.

Next we describe the 526 parents, the 391 children from China, as well as the 121 other children who live in these 361 households. The following sections include data from the study.

The Parents

Who are the parents that responded to the invitation to participate in the study? As is shown in Table 3.1, the majority of the parents filling out the questionnaires were mothers. Most par-

Table 3.1
Sample Description of Adoptive Parents (N = 526)

Variable	Descriptive Statistic
Age (median)	42.7 years

Family role
  Mother
  Father
	
	68%
	32%

Household size (median and range)	3.4 (2 to 8 persons)
Group Caucasian	 96%
Marital status Currently married	 81%

Education
  Up to four years of college
  Post graduate study
	
	35%
	65%

Household income (median)	$70,000 to $89,999

Employment status
  Fathers (working full time)
  Mothers (working full time)
  Mothers (working part time)
	
	92%
	53%
	29%

FCC member	81%
Has a religious preference	80%

ents were currently married. We strongly discouraged parents from filling out their questionnaires jointly, and instead offered to mail separate questionnaires to their spouses or partners. Those parents who did complete questionnaires were 32 percent fathers and 68 percent mothers. The overrepresentation of mothers in the sample most likely reflects both single women who were able to adopt, as well as the acceptance of traditional gender roles in which mothers take more responsibility for children.

The parents in our sample were older than the typical "first-time" biological parent. On average, the adoptive parents were in their early forties. Mothers averaged forty-two years of age and fathers averaged forty-four years. These older ages suggest that these parents were further along in their careers and would have higher incomes than what we might otherwise expect of new parents.

Their jobs were highly diverse. Examples include physician, accountant, social worker, high school teacher, nurse, engineer, journalist, management consultant, librarian, artist, writer, banker, lawyer, and professor. Thus, they worked in the health field as doctors and nurses, and in education as kindergarten and high school teachers, as guidance counselors, as principals, and as college professors. They worked in social services as clinical social workers and for adoption agencies. They worked in retail and in communications, and also in technical fields such as computer graphics and as software engineers. They were self-employed in small businesses and also as freelance writers and artists. These occupations suggest a heavy prior involvement in career.

The vast majority of the fathers worked for pay. Mothers were significantly more likely than fathers to report that they were *not* currently working for pay (18 percent versus 2 percent). Fifty-three percent of the mothers were working full time compared with 92 percent of the fathers, although the proportion of single mothers who were working full time (93 percent) was slightly higher than fathers.

As would be expected from the occupational descriptions, the parents who participated in the survey tended to be relatively affluent. Since we asked not about the income of individuals but about the entire household, we will defer presentation of these data until the section on household characteristics. However, we did inquire about the educational attainment of each parent.

When asked how much education they had, the vast majority of parents reported at least some college education, and most (65 percent) had engaged in postgraduate study. The level of educational attainment in the study sample is far in excess of the general population.

Although there is only minimal variation among the parents in education and income, there is much ethnic diversity. The ethnic heterogeneity of the United States created by past immigration is reflected in the self-reports of parents about their own "main ethnic origins." Parents report being Armenian, Australian, Canadian, Irish, Italian, Scottish, Spanish, Ukrainian, Portuguese, Russian, Jewish, Polish, Dutch, Swedish, and Slovakian, among many others. Parents also reported many combinations, such as French-English, German-Polish, Irish-Dutch, Swiss-English, and Polish-Russian. These are reports by individual parents; there is even greater ethnic diversity within households. Most parents were Caucasian (96 percent), but the sample also included a small number of persons identifying themselves as Chinese, African American, or Japanese.

The ethnic diversity implies that the families with children from China are multicultural in theory (if not in general practice) rather than bi-cultural. Although most of these parents are descendants of immigrants who were brought up to assimilate, many will follow the model of cultural pluralsm in parenting their adoptive children.

There was also substantial variation in religion. When asked for their religious preference, parents reported being Protestant (32 percent), Catholic (21 percent), or Jewish (13 percent), and about 14 percent cited other religious orientations. About 20 percent reported no religious preference.

The Children

Who are the children in these 361 adoptive families? We asked parents from where in the PRC their children were adopted. As is shown in Table 3.2, 360 families reported that at the time of the adoption(s) their 390 children were living in 14 different provinces and 1 municipality. (The remaining family reported adopting one Chinese newborn from a Chinese couple living in

Table 3.2
Where Do the 390 Children Adopted in China Come From?

Province/Municipality*	Total	First Adoption	Second Adoption
Hunan	64	60	4
Jiangsu	63	57	6
Jiangxi	58	54	4
Guangdong	43	38	5
Anhui	41	41	-
Hubei	41	38	3
Zhejiang	34	32	2
Guangxi	14	13	1
Fujian	11	10	1
Sichuan	7	6	1
Yunnan	5	4	1
Shanghai	5	3	2
Shaanxi	2	2	-
Guizhou	1	1	-
Hebei	1	1	-
Total	390	360	30**

Notes: *One of the 361 families adopted a baby born to Chinese parents living in the United States, rather than adopting from a province or municipality in China.
**Includes one family counted as both a second and a third adoption.

the United States.) Most of the orphanages are located in urban areas, but it is widely believed that a majority of the children come from rural areas—not too far away. The vast majority of the children will have no conscious memories of what their local area looked like, what dialect was spoken, what food was served, how people earned their living, how and where people shopped, or any other aspect of everyday life.

As can be seen in Table 3.3, out of the 512 children listed in these 361 households, 391 (76.4 percent) were adopted from China, 2.7 percent from the United States, 1.2 percent from Korea, Thailand, or Peru, and 19.7 percent were the biological children of either the mother, the father, or both.

Table 3.3 shows a vast difference in the proportion of daughters between the children adopted from China and the other children in these families. The biological children are much more likely to be sons than are the other children. The presence of sons in the family may be one reason leading parents to China where mostly girls are available for adoption. The biological children in these households also tended to be older than their siblings from China.

At the time of the study, the average age of the children adopted from China was 2.1 years; the youngest were between 5

Table 3.3
Numbers and Characteristics of the 512 Children in the 361 Families

Children	Adopted from			Biological
	China	*Korea, Thailand, Peru*	*U.S.A.*	
Number	391	6	14	101
Age (mean years)	2.1	6.3	5.4	10.3
Sex (% female)	97.4	83.3	64.3	39.6

and 6 months and the oldest were 7 years old. More than 97 percent were girls. It was no surprise to find that the vast majority of the children adopted from China were girls because, as already noted, the abandoned children in China are almost all females. What was surprising is that as many as 10 of the Chinese children were boys.

A total of 249 of the 391 children from China have no siblings; thus, 64 percent are "only children." A total of 29 children have Chinese sisters adopted from China. The children adopted from China have 121 non-Chinese siblings living with them.

Where in the United States were these children living? The U.S. destinations encompassed 38 states. As is shown in Table 3.4, the destinations of the adopted children in our sample were concentrated in Massachusetts, California, New York, and Ohio. But children from China also went to homes in Vermont, Utah, and North Dakota—places that have less of a recent history of Asian

Table 3.4
Regional Distribution of Adoptive Homes (N = 360)*

Area	States	% (# of homes)
Massachusetts		27% (96 homes)
Midwest	IA, IL, IN, KS, MI, MN, MO, MT, ND, NE, OH, WI	22% (80 homes)
Other Northeastern	CT, ME, NH, NJ, NY, PA, RI, VT	19% (67 homes)
California		11% (40 homes)
Southern	AL, DC, FL, GA, MD, NC, VA, WV	10% (37 homes)
Northwest	AK, OR, WA	6% (21 homes)
Southwest	AZ, CO, NM, TX, UT	5% (19 homes)

Note: *One family was currently living outside the United States.

immigration. The provinces the girls and boys were adopted from are described in chapter 4.

The Households

At the time the 361 families completed their questionnaires, 332 had adopted one child from China; 28 families had adopted two children from China; and one family had adopted three children. Household incomes were especially high; 21 percent reported household income over $130,000 in 1995. Median household income was $70,000. Most children lived in a two-parent household, but some 15.5 percent lived in single-parent households, with the vast majority of these in mother-headed households. Households consisted of 2 to 8 people ranging from households with a single mother and an adopted daughter to larger households that included biological children in addition to a mother and a father and, in some cases, extended family. A small number of the households also included unrelated others.

This section has only described households. It is possible that an unknown number of parents have children from previous marriages, or grown children from the current marriage, who live elsewhere.

REASONS FOR ADOPTION

Before turning to the study data, we provide some background about the recent developments in the United States that have led many American parents to adopt children internationally. Since *Roe v. Wade* legalized abortion in 1973 in the United States, there has been a dramatic decrease in the number of healthy infants who are available for adoption. As a result, it has become more difficult to adopt domestically. Recent legal decisions associated with "open adoption" have also made some prospective adoptive parents wary about the permanence of the adoption and the reappearance of birth parents. In addition, the empowering of birth parents to participate in choosing the adoptive parents has made it more difficult for older or unmarried adults to adopt. For these reasons, some prospective adoptive parents in the United States are turning to international adoptions, and China has become an increasingly popular source constituting more than a fifth of all international adoptions into the United States by the mid 1990s.

Previous studies show age, childlessness, and the resources needed to support the adoption are associated with the propensity to adopt in the United States (Bachrach et al., 1991). This would lead us to expect that the persons who desire a parenting experience and turn to adoption in China would also tend to be older, without children, and relatively affluent.

Our data show that these factors are indeed salient for study parents, who, as expected, tended to be older and more affluent than more traditional first-time biological parents. The fact that 71 percent listed an infertility problem as a reason for adoption also suggests that childlessness was a motivating factor for many of the study parents. Although we did not ask explicitly about the link between adoption and household income, our results clearly support this association.

Table 3.5 shows the mean (or average) scores for the sixteen reasons for choosing adoption as a way to create or expand a family. The most important reasons parents gave for adopting are shown above the double line. Parents gave the highest ratings to wanting a baby, wanting to have a parenting experience, wanting to pass on values to the next generation, and wanting to provide opportunities for a child that the parent did not have. These reasons received scores that, on average, are between "somewhat" and "very" important.

By contrast, the factors below the double line scored between "not at all" and "a little" important. The least important factors were pressure from peers and family. It may be that when there is

Table 3.5
Reasons for Adopting: Rank-Ordered by Importance

Thinking back to your decision to adopt, how important were each of the following factors:	Mean
wanting a baby?	3.66
wanting to have a parenting experience?	3.41
an infertility problem?	2.71
wanting to pass on your values to the next generation?	2.57
wanting to provide a child with opportunities that you didn't have?	2.41
wanting to have someone to count on emotionally as you get older?	1.79
not wanting to add to the world's population?	1.75
wanting to give another child a sibling?	1.66
not wanting to live alone?	1.42
wanting to have someone to take care of you as you get older?	1.37
wanting someone to fulfill your unrealized dreams?	1.35
wanting someone to carry on your family name?	1.31
desire for an older child?	1.29
family pressure?	1.16
wanting to have someone to count on financially as you get older?	1.12
pressure from your peers?	1.06

Note: Response Categories: 1 = not at all important; 2 = a little important; 3 = somewhat important; 4 = very important.

pressure put upon adults to have children—it is only for the bearing of biological offspring. Family and friends may not influence decisions to choose adoption as a way of forming a family. Although not important to most parents, some families with a biological child or a child adopted from another country were also motivated by a desire to find a sibling for their other child.

Other factors thought to be *not important* were wanting to have someone to count on financially as the parent gets older, wanting someone to carry on the family name, wanting to have someone to take care of the parent as he or she gets older, and wanting someone to fulfill unrealized dreams. Although apparently unimportant to American adoptive parents, many of these factors may be important reasons for married persons in China seeking to adopt.

About one third of all the parents were planning at the time of the survey to adopt another child from China. But, as of 1997, the China Center for Adoption Affairs had imposed more stringent requirements for persons wanting to adopt a second child, including that second adoptions be limited to older children and/or children with special needs. As a result, some of these adoptive parents may have turned to other countries to further expand their families.

REASONS FOR CHOOSING CHINA

Prospective parents turn to China for a variety of reasons. Eligibility requirements may tip the decision toward China, by virtue of its liberal policies toward single parents (China allows single men and women to adopt) and toward *older* first-time prospective parents (prospective parents must be at least 35 years of age to be eligible). Some other countries accept married couples only and require that parents be younger. Also, the potential for adopting a *healthy* infant or toddler is generally perceived as greater in China than in the United States. In some cases, parents may have personal connections to China such as having studied or worked there. More rarely, the parents may be (or are married to) second- or third-generation Chinese immigrants themselves. In summary, eligibility, health status of prospective children, and cultural and personal interests may all be involved, among other factors, in leading one to adopt in China.

As already noted, one of the reasons prospective parents choose to adopt internationally is the undersupply of healthy infants relative to the number of individuals and couples seeking to adopt. In fact, as Table 3.6 indicates, the number one reason given by adoptive parents for deciding to adopt from China is "the availability of healthy children." Three quarters of the parents said that the availability of healthy children was a "very important" factor when they decided to adopt from China. This is followed closely by meeting eligibility requirements and a humanistic desire to give a child a family. Also important, as expected, was feeling secure that birth parents could not change their minds, the quickness of the adoption process—more than one half of the parents reported that there was less than six months between thinking about adopting their first child from China and their home study—and, finally, the perceived low risk of fetal alcohol syndrome, drug abuse, or AIDS.

Below the line in Table 3.6 are the least important reasons for choosing to adopt from China. Least important as reasons for choosing to adopt from China were believing a Chinese child would be easier to raise, believing a Chinese child would be more intelligent than a child of another ethnicity, and knowing other families who adopted from China. The latter factor may become more important in the future if the number of families with children from China continues to increase.

FURTHER OBSERVATIONS ABOUT THE STUDY

The data in this book are based only on a single survey. At best, it provides a cross-sectional snapshot, but the theoretical issues really invite a longitudinal study which tracks children and families over a long period of time.

Table 3.6
Reasons for Choosing to Adopt from China

When you decided to adopt from China, how important were each of the following factors:	Mean
availability of healthy children?	3.68
meeting eligibility requirements?	3.39
desire to give a child a family?	3.38
feeling secure that birth parents could not change their mind?	3.21
the quickness of the adoption process?	3.16
low risk of fetal alchohol syndrome, drug abuse, or AIDS?	3.11
wanting a child of a specific age?	3.06
interest in Chinese culture?	2.85
not wanting to deal with birth parents?	2.77
liking the appearance of Chinese children?	2.38
recommendation of adoption agency?	2.05
the opportunity to visit China?	2.02
knowing other families who adopted from China?	1.99
believing a Chinese child would be more intelligent than a child of another ethnicity?	1.39
believing a Chinese child would be easier to raise?	1.27

Note: Response Categories: 1 = not at all important; 2 = a little important; 3 = somewhat important; 4 = very important.

There are several other limitations of the study methodology that need to be acknowledged. First, the sample was not randomly drawn from the population of American parents with children from China. Since all respondents volunteered to participate in the study, we have no way of knowing the characteristics of adoptive parents who heard about the study but chose not to volunteer or the characteristics of adoptive parents who never heard about the study. The sample may overrepresent parents with more interest in bi-cultural socialization. Also, and as already noted, fathers are underrepresented in the sample.

A further concern arises from the unknown biases inherent in choosing a sample in such diverse ways. For example, how parents heard about the study was associated with the section of the United States in which they lived. Parents in the northeastern states were more likely to have heard about the study through a FCC newsletter or flyer, where as parents from other parts of the country were more likely to hear about the study through the Internet. However, parents who heard about the study in different ways did not differ significantly in their attitudes toward bi-cultural socialization.

Given that there was no possible way when we began our study to obtain a random sample of the total population of parents who adopt from China, we believe that the approach taken was a reasonable one. Indeed, the sample has a number of strengths. The sample is geographically and demographically diverse. Families come from thirty-eight states. Participants include both mothers and (some) fathers, one and two parent households, and a sizeable number of families with non-Asian siblings.

It was probably an advantage that many of the children were infants and toddlers, as it enabled us to measure parental attitudes just as their families were forming. Parents provided rich qualitative as well as quantitative data during a period when their decisions to adopt internationally were still easily recalled and their ideas about bi-cultural socialization were still in the process of being formed.

In the next chapter, we turn from the West to the East and describe the birth country and culture that the children adopted from China leave behind.

Chapter 4

THE BIRTH COUNTRY

Our intention in this chapter is to bring to life what is traditionally meant by "growing up the Chinese way" in China, while also highlighting the limited possibilities of Chinese socialization in America. We attempt to point out both the general and specific cultural aspects of the children's birth country that need to be considered when deciding whether and how to provide the children with a cultural biography. Thus, in addition to describing parental experiences and satisfaction with their trips, we provide a general introduction to the social history and culture of the PRC.

We begin by putting the adoptions into the social and political context of the PRC. A major challenge for adoptive parents will occur when their children want to know what led them to leave their birth country and to be adopted by Americans. An important part of the answer to the question "How did I become part of this family" can only be found in the contemporary history of China's efforts to control its fertility and the advent of the *one-child policy* which created the need and the opportunity for foreign adoption. From the standpoint of many adoptive parents, explaining the one-child policy is perhaps the only time that the contemporary politics of the PRC will enter into discussions of the child's Chinese heritage.

CHINA'S ONE-CHILD POLICY AND ITS CONSEQUENCES

China's 1990 census indicated a population of 1.18 billion people (Reist, 1995), although by the end of 1996, the PRC reported a population of 1.22 billion people. The actual population size is probably higher. Even if one accepts the official estimate, the implication is that one out of every four people in the world is living in China (Hertsgaard, 1997). Although the PRC and the United States are roughly comparable in size, China has only one fifth as much arable land and four times as many people to feed.

Until recently, the PRC has had a totalitarian regime with immense power residing in the central government. Government control touched virtually every aspect of personal life, including reproduction. Decreasing the growth of the population has been a concern of the central government since 1955, when the first of several birth control campaigns began. In an effort to curb the rapid population growth that took place in the 1960s and 1970s, China tried various approaches to population control, including strongly encouraging later ages at marriage, longer spacing between births, and having fewer children (*wan, xi, shao*). When these strategies failed to produce the desired effect, the controversial one-child policy was implemented in 1979.

It was in response to this official policy, and its often harsh implementation, that some Chinese families chose to abandon infants and toddlers in public places.

The agents of the one-child policy go far beyond propaganda: the policy is linked to techniques of campaign mobilization at every level of organizational structure in which citizens of China are involved. Women are empowered through women's associations to monitor other women's menstruation cycles, pregnancies, and birth control usage, and to administer rewards and disincentives. Intense social pressure is used to persuade women to abort unscheduled pregnancies. Intense persuasion often turns into coercion when cadres get carried away with their missions. Both forced abortions and forced sterilizations have resulted from excessive zeal. In general, however, the program is contributing to the downward trend in birth rates. (Soled, 1995, p. 240)

If China's one-child policy worked as intended, then one would not expect to find a surplus of children of either gender available for adoption. But coexisting with this one-child policy is the traditional preference for sons in Chinese culture. This preference for sons is still strong in economically underdeveloped rural areas of China where there are no equivalents of social security or pension programs. Many Chinese parents perceive their economic futures as dependent on having a son who will take care of them in their old age. A daughter will "marry away," becoming a member of her husband's family, where she will be expected to support her in-laws when they grow old. There are also powerful cultural reasons: For example, without a son the family name will die, and, in a patriarchal society, sons by definition are more valued than girls. Although traditional Chinese culture is strongly pronatal, the birth of a son is viewed as a "big happiness" whereas the birth of a daughter is viewed as only a "small happiness."

Given these economic and cultural factors, what choices were open to women when they gave birth to baby girls in the face of such intense social and cultural pressures to have sons? One possible choice was infanticide which had a cultural history in certain parts of China as a means of family planning. Another alternative was to forego the possibility of having a son, or to suffer the economic and social penalties imposed on parents who had a second or third daughter. Or before giving birth, the family could bribe a doctor to use the technology of ultrasound B machines for prenatal sex identification and then to perform an abortion if the fetus were a girl. Although abortion is legal, the use of ultrasound to determine the sex of the fetus is illegal. In any case, access to the ultrasound B technology is mostly limited to urban residents who have the state health plan and/or those who can afford to pay for it privately. A final option was to abandon female babies, which is also illegal. This is the avenue that has led to baby girls in orphanages who become available for international adoption.

Sara Dorow describes this process in a story book designed for children adopted from China. When reading her description, recall that in China abandoned babies are legally considered to be orphans.

Like many other families in China at the time, your family made a very painful decision that another family should take care of you. But China did not have an easy way to help families make an adoption plan. Your parents could get in trouble if they took you straight to an orphanage. So they bundled you up, and maybe put a note in your pocket telling when you were born and explaining that they wanted so much for a family to give you the kind of love and care they couldn't provide. They then carried you to a public place, like a park, or a busy street corner, or a police station—a place where they knew you would be found by people who could take care of you. And that is exactly what happened! Someone quickly found you and took you to the police station, because the police would know how to help. There a police officer wrote down information about when and where you were found and then took you to an orphanage, where there were nurses and beds and warm food. (1997, pp. 18–19)

International adoptions are occurring disproportionately in provinces that are contiguous to or south of the Yangtzi River (the Chinese people call it *Changjiang*) which runs through southeastern China. Reflecting this tendency, relatively few of the children in the current study came from provinces located in northern China or from provinces located in the far southwest (see Table 3.2).

The nonrandom distribution of children available for adoption across different provinces suggests that there are more factors than just the one-child policy and the preference for sons involved in decisions to abandon baby girls. Cultural, economic, and political factors may also be involved, as well as differential population size and fertility. Another factor may be birth order. Rural areas have a de facto one son (families who have a first-born son are subject to the one-child policy) or two-children policy (if the first-born is a daughter, families may try again for a son). Thus, when the second child is another daughter, this child may be abandoned, suggesting that many of the abandoned girls may have had biological siblings (Johnson, 1998).

The recent abandonments of baby girls may also represent a traditional cultural response to major social changes. In the 1990s, these changes involved privatization of state-owned enterprises, the decentralization of power, migration from rural to urban areas, and unprecedented economic development. It is well known that modernization is linked to the desire for smaller families. Smaller families in contemporary rural China typically mean 2, 3, or 4 children, rather than 10 to 12 as in earlier eras.

The desire for smaller families implies that selection for boys becomes even more intense. Although it seems harsh to Americans, for some rural Chinese families who feel they need sons to continue the family line, to work on the household farm, and to assure security in old age, abandonment of baby girls represents a form of family planning and a positive alternative to infanticide. For social as well as economic reasons, handicapped children are particularly at risk of being abandoned regardless of their sex and whether they are from the city or the country. Many Chinese families feel shamed by handicapped progeny.

China's one-child policy has evolved and changed since 1979, to the extent that some observers question whether, in fact, a uniform policy ever existed (Fong and Gusukuma, 1998). Despite the great power residing in the central government, exceptions to the one-child policy abound, reflecting the strength of traditional Chinese values and culture to shape policy. In general, the policy is more lenient in the countryside where Chinese families are permitted to have a second child if their first was a girl. There is also evidence of a recent relaxation of the one-child rule in medium-size cities where persuasion and economic disincentives have replaced the harsher coercion of the 1980s (Faison, 1997). Nonetheless, so long as reducing population growth by limiting family size remains a major goal of the PRC, along with the preference for sons, abandonments of baby girls are likely to continue.

GROWTH IN ADOPTIONS BY AMERICANS

About ten years after the implementation of the one-child policy, baby girls began to be adopted by United States citizens. At first, adoptions were arranged directly and informally

through the local orphanages, but later the process was central-
ized in Beijing. Table 4.1 shows the growth in adoptions by U.S.
citizens from China since 1989 in terms of federal fiscal years
(October to September). The numbers are based on visas given
by the U.S. State Department and reveal the great increases in
adoptions of Chinese (mostly) girls into the United States dur-

Table 4.1
**Statistics on Number of Adoptions by Year: Counts of
Immigration and Naturalization Service (INS) Immigrant
Visas as Reported by the Department of State by Government
Fiscal Year (October 1–September 30)**

Year	INS Visas	Comment
1989	201	Ad hoc private adoptions
1990	29	Ad hoc private adoptions
1991	61	Ad hoc private adoptions
1992	206	Chinese National People's Congress approved the Adoption Law, which led to the establishment of the China Center for Adoption Affairs. Adoptions permitted by persons over 35 and childless, married or unmarried.
1993	330	Moratorium on adoption begins as lines of authority involving the Ministries of Justice and Civil Affairs are reorganized.
1994	787	Adoptions resume with second adoptions and adoptions by families with other children permitted.
1995	2130	December 1995. Human Rights Watch Report, "Death by Default." Adoptions processing continues, but orphanages are closed to foreign visitors.
1996	3333	Ministry of Civil Affairs assumes full responsibility for the adoption process. By the end of the fiscal year a return to stricter policies for adoptions.
1997	3553	Adoptions continue to increase in spite of the stricter policies.
Total	10,630	1989–1997

ing the 1990s. Ad hoc private adoptions refer to adoptions before 1992 in which the Chinese central government was not
importantly involved. Instead the locally funded orphanages
were the decision makers.

The passage of the PRC Adoption Law and the creation of
the Center for Adoption Affairs in 1992 formalized and central-
ized the process of adopting Chinese babies internationally to
the point that officials in Beijing became involved in assigning
prospective parents to specific orphanages and specific children,
and establishing a uniform payment schedule to compensate the
orphanages for the care given to the children. The Adoption
Law offered opportunities to prospective American parents over
thirty-five years of age, married or unmarried, so long as the
couple was childless (children from a previous marriage were
usually not considered in determining whether the *couple* was
childless) or willing to accept a handicapped child. Although in
the past adoptions did take place in the PRC (mostly between
members of the same family), since the implementation of the
one-child policy individual families are not allowed legally to put
a child up for adoption.

In Fiscal Year (FY) 1993 adoptions reached 330 even though
a moratorium was declared around the end of April. Chinese officials refused to give a reason or say how long it would last
("China Calls a Halt," 1993). But the moratorium was most
likely linked to an internal conflict about lines of authority between the Ministry of Justice and the Ministry of Civil Affairs.
The timing of the moratorium also coincided with China's em-
barrassment over the article entitled "China's Market in Orphan
Girls" that appeared prominently in the *New York Times Magazine* section in early April (Porter, 1993). When adoptions re-
sumed after a hiatus of one year, there occurred a great increase
in the number of Chinese girls adopted by U.S. parents. For the
first time, parents were allowed to adopt a second Chinese child

and adoptions by families with other children were now permitted.

In calendar year 1995, the Human Rights Watch Report entitled "Death by Default" upset the Chinese government by alleging that its one-child policy was leading to mass infanticide of infant girls. (Allegations of infanticide were based on the large gap between expected numbers of female births and actual registered births of Chinese girls.) In apparent response to the Human Rights Watch Report and other allegations about "dying rooms" and the poor conditions of life in some orphanages, the Chinese government opted to close the orphanages to foreign visitors (including adoptive parents) but not to stop international adoptions.

By FY 1995, adoptions of Chinese girls were accounting for about 22 percent of all international adoptions into the United States, and had come to represent the single largest source of adoptions from abroad. The United States was also the major, although not the sole, destination of Chinese orphaned girls. By FY 1996, it appeared that the Chinese were, once again, beginning to reevaluate their adoption policy and discouraging second adoptions, as well as adoptions by parents with children from prior marriages (or relationships). In spite of these stricter policies, adoptions increased in 1997 to 3,553. In September, the last month of FY 1997, there were 447 adoptions of Chinese children by American parents, which was the highest monthly total ever recorded by the office of the U.S. Consulate in Guangzhou.

The study parents reported adopting in China in the *calendar years* (January–December) 1991 to 1996. Similar to the pattern reported above in terms of *fiscal years* (October–September), there were few adoptions in the early years, but they increased dramatically in the mid-1990s. These also included the growth of second adoptions as these became permitted by the PRC in 1994. There were only 6 adoptions by the study parents in 1991 and 24 adoptions in each of the years 1992 and 1993. By 1994, there were 117 adoptions (including 8 second adoptions), and in 1995, there were 225 adoptions (including 21 second adoptions).

There were 138 adoptions reported by study parents during 1996 (including 11 second adoptions). The apparent decline reflects the fact that data collection, which began in June of that year, concluded in October, and thus did not cover all of 1996. A few parents who had anticipated taking part in the study became ineligible to participate because they were still waiting for their dossiers to be approved by the Center for Adoption Affairs in Beijing, which in 1996 was undergoing a bureaucratic reorganization. (Parents had to have returned from China with their child by October to be eligible for the study.)

The next section summarizes the experiences of the 360 families in adopting in China. Their journeys were organized by several U.S. adoption agencies with international programs, and in this way may be viewed as a cross-section of experiences.

THE ADOPTIVE PARENTS IN CHINA

Table 4.2 presents study data about the personal experiences in China of the parents. Not surprisingly, given China's requirement that at least one parent travel, 94 percent of the parents who completed questionnaires traveled to China. Parents traveled to as many as fifteen (out of thirty) provinces and autonomous regions in the PRC. The majority of their travel time was spent in the province where they adopted their children. When one of two parents did not travel, the decision was often related to needing to take care of another child or children already at home.

The median length of stay in China was twelve days, with a typical trip beginning with one to two days in Hong Kong, then a week in the province in which the child's orphanage was lo-

Table 4.2
Parents' First Adoption Experience in China (N = 526)

Traveled to China for the adoption (% yes)	94.1
Length of stay in China during the adoption (median)	12 days
Traveled with a group (% yes)	89.8
Is still in touch with members of a group (% yes)	96.8
Age of child at first meeting (median)	7 months
Visited the orphanage (% yes)	54.7
Average rating of the orphanage (1 = inferior to 7 = superior)	4.9
Met with the person(s) who cared for the child (% yes)	86.1
Given the opportunity to keep in touch with the caregivers (% yes)	54.9
Stayed in touch with the caregiver when given the chance (% yes)	56.4

cated, followed by a stay of two to three days in Guangzhou to apply for an entrance visa from the American consulate so that the child could enter the United States. Most of the prospective parents traveled with a group of other adoptive parents, and were met in China by a bilingual liaison as described in chapter 2. For most travelers, the group experience appears to have been meaningful, as an extremely high proportion (97 percent) reported at the time of the study that they have stayed in touch with other group members since returning to the United States.

Asking parents to evaluate the orphanages turned out to be a difficult research task. One problem was that, as human rights issues came more and more to the forefront, parents began to be denied permission to visit the orphanages. When asked whether they visited the orphanages, about 55 percent reported that they did, but this was for the most part a matter of opportunity since, as noted, orphanages were closed to visits from foreigners in 1995.

In addition, many parents who did visit the orphanage responded to this question with the marginal comment "compared to what?" This criticism of the question was well taken, but we reasoned that there would be at least as many problems introduced by specifying a comparative yardstick. The measurement of this issue was further complicated by the fact that an unknown number of parents may have based their ratings on foster care rather than orphanage care, athough virtually all foster care was administratively associated with an orphanage. Even with these limitations, the data are among the first to systematically draw on the actual experiences of American parents adopting a child in China.

Those 475 parents who provided ratings of the orphanages rated the orphanages above the midpoint on a 7 point scale where 1 = inferior and 7 = superior. The overall mean was 4.9, and none of the 15 provinces received a rating lower than 4.4. It is important to note in this regard that a province can have more than one orphanage, as well as different foster care arrangements.

Regardless of whether they were able to tour the orphanage, most parents met the person(s) who cared for their child, although 19 percent did not. One can imagine the limited opportunity for communication, given a single bilingual liaison and the needs of a whole group of parents and children. Even so, more than half of the parents who met a caregiver reported that they were given the opportunity to keep in touch, and a majority of these actually did so. Presumably such correspondence also required that bilingual resources be available to the parents in the United States or to the caregivers in China.

Satisfaction with Travel Experiences in China

Theoretically, one might anticipate that the more satisfied parents were with their experiences in China, the more they would want to keep their child connected to her birth country and culture. Thus, we asked parents ten questions about how satisfied they were with different aspects of their adoption experiences in China. Results are shown in Table 4.3 for those 496 parents who traveled.

As Table 4.3 indicates, the highest satisfaction rating was given to "how the parent was treated by the Chinese man or woman on the street." The second highest rating was for "how the parent was treated by Chinese officials." These positive ratings may have reflected the support within China being given to international adoption in the 1990s. Not surprisingly, parents were *least satisfied* with the amount of information they received about their adopted child (61 percent were "not at all" satisfied or just "a little" satisfied), and the opportunities to meet with

Table 4.3
Satisfaction* with Travel Experiences in China (N = 496)

Overall, how satisfied were you with each of the following aspects of your trip(s) to China:	Mean
how you were treated by the Chinese "man" or "woman" "on the street"?	3.69
how you were treated by Chinese officials?	3.53
how physically comfortable you were in your travels?	3.30
the opportunities you had to get a sense of China?	3.26
the amount of help you were given in caring for your child?	3.08
how much money you needed to spend?	3.00
opportunities to visit Chinese landmarks?	2.98
opportunities to learn about Chinese culture?	2.93
opportunities to meet with the people who cared for your child?	2.63
the amount of information you received about your adoptive child?	2.28

Note: *Parents could check one of four response categories. The responses and their values are: 1 = not at all satisfied, 2 = a little satisfied, 3 = somewhat satisfied; 4 = very satisfied.

the people who cared for the child (45 percent were "not at all" satisfied or just "a little" satisfied). Again this probably reflects parents' frustrations with the limited opportunities to meet one-on-one with caregivers, and when contact did take place, the two-way frustrations in trying to communicate across a major language barrier.

Parents who had traveled twice to adopt children from China were asked to comment on any differences between their two trips. Responses were quite varied, but all noticed some differences between the first trip and the second trip. Among the factors cited as differentiating one trip from another were unexpected illnesses, lack of opportunity to visit the orphanage, limited or enhanced opportunities for tourism, increases or decreases in the efficiency of the process, differences in facilitator styles, or group versus individual travel.

The following comment by a parent who traveled twice notes the pluses and minuses connected to each trip: "Our group was much bigger the second time (11 children) vs. the first time (3 children); in addition the regulations had changed so that we met our children in the hotel rather than the orphanage. Things were more streamlined and efficient the second time, but in some ways were more fun the first time. Still both trips had their high points and I enjoyed both in different ways." Another parent's comments reflected the changing opportunities to visit the orphanage: "We visited our first daughter's orphanage which was good. We were not allowed to visit our second daughter's orphanage (the rules changed) or her village (too far from the city we were staying in). I wished we could have."

A summary measure of overall satisfaction was also constructed that used all ten items and that has a reliability coefficient (Cronbach's alpha) of .770. The average of the overall satisfaction scale is 3.07 or just over "somewhat satisfied." Using this summary measure, we tested for differences between mothers and fathers in the same family with respect to satisfaction, but found no significant difference in overall satisfaction. There was a significant association between parental age and overall satisfaction; as age went up, satisfaction with the trip(s) went down.

Satisfaction with the adoption trip to China tended to be higher in those provinces to which fewer adoptive parents (in the current study) traveled. One interpretation is that adoptive parents might have received the most attention in those provinces where foreign adoption was still a novelty. By contrast, where foreign adoptions had become commonplace, the process as well as the experience may have been more bureaucratized. Opportunity for tourism may also have contributed to the observed differences in parents' satisfaction.

SOCIALIZATION TO CHINESE CULTURE

Adoptive parents who choose to educate their children about China have much to become acquainted with that cannot be learned in one or two trips. China's history, unlike that of the United States, goes back at least four thousand years (Abraham, 1995). "China is the longest-running show on earth. Countries have come and gone, empires have risen and fallen, but China lives on. It has done so for thousands of years" (Summerfield, 1979, p. v). For example, circa 145–87 B.C.E., the Chinese scholar Sima Qian began a written chronicle of the biographical histories of the royal dynasties in the Chinese language that can still be read today (Abraham, 1995). Chinese poetry and literature also go back thousands of years. *Shijing*, the first collection of Chinese poems, is believed to have been written around 1100 B.C.E.

Up through the beginning of this century, irrespective of regime, political system, differences in local customs or dialects, life for most Chinese people went on with very little change, and children's lives were not very different from their ancestors' lives

(Spence and Chin, 1996). There was much uniformity in Chinese *culture* even though there was little idea of citizenship or nationhood until the twentieth century. Thus, culture rather than political boundaries and citizenship is what identifies "Chinese-ness." The written language is the same everywhere that Chinese is spoken regardless of local dialect. Holidays such as the Chinese New Year (*Chun Jie*) and the Mid-Autumn Festival (*Zhong Qiu Jie*) are celebrated wherever Chinese people live, whether on the Mainland, Taiwan, Singapore, Indonesia, Thailand, or even Brazil.

Asian cultures are strictly structured by authority, and children are raised to know their part in the hierarchy. Children raised "the Chinese way" are expected to control their impulses; to conform; to respect the authority of their superiors, including their parents, grandparents, and teachers; to accept discipline; to focus on what's good for the family; and to achieve academically. The ultimate goal is to achieve honor for the family rather than for the individual. Conversely, if children do not achieve, the family is shamed. Because family honor is at stake, children tend to work hard and to respect authority both at home as well as in school. Thus, in adolescence, Chinese children appear to be less rebellious, less delinquent, and more disciplined than their American counterparts (S. Lau, 1996).

Being pious, loyal to family, modest about personal achievement, valuing the family over the individual, and respecting the importance of ancestors are embedded in everyday life for persons who grow up the Chinese way. In a book intended to help American social workers better understand Chinese-American families, the hierarchical structure of family relationships was described in the following terms:

> The decision maker in a Chinese family is usually the husband or the oldest male or female in the household. This traditional hierarchy, based on age and gender, is

explicitly sanctioned by Confucian ethics, which have been practiced widely in one form or another for more than 2,000 years in the Chinese-speaking world and define what is considered to be morally proper behavior within the family. Failure to adhere to these moral standards can be very disruptive in traditionally oriented families. (Elliott et al., 1996, p. 99)

Rather than emphasize Confucian beliefs, many adoptive parents choose to emphasize Chinese cultural celebrations. The most important of these is the Spring Festival, which is also known as the Chinese New Year. Because the Chinese use a lunar rather than a solar calendar, the date is not synonymous with New Year's Day as celebrated in the West. The celebration of the Chinese New Year traditionally lasts fifteen days, ending with the Lantern Festival. There are regional differences as to how the holiday is celebrated; for example, Northerners associate the holiday with making dumplings and Southerners with making glutinous rice cakes.

But, despite regional differences, the traditions of wishing for peace and prosperity in the coming year and performing ceremonies that honor the family's ancestors are broadly shared. Traditionally, preparation starts long before New Year's Eve. Every Chinese family does a thorough housecleaning, makes or buys new clothes for family members, and does extensive New Year's shopping to stock the kitchen with various ingredients for making traditional dishes for the New Year's Eve dinner. Preparation for the holiday also includes "sweetening the Kitchen Gods" with *zaotang* (a special Chinese candy) seven days before the New Year, and hanging scrolls with verses meaningful to the family that are often drawn by specially talented and respected calligraphers on a red paper using gold or black ink.

The New Year's Eve dinner is the way that the family (traditionally the extended family included many generations living under the same roof) begins the celebration of the holiday. A large whole fish symbolizes the abundance that is hoped for during the coming year and is a "must" for every family's New Year's Eve dinner. All members of the family feel obligated to be present, if at all possible, for this dinner. In rural areas, married daughters are obligated to be present at the New Year's Eve dinner with their husband's family, but the couple is also expected to pay a visit to the wife's family during the first five days of the holiday.

On New Year's Eve, the celebration also includes lighting red lanterns as it begins to get dark and setting off fire crackers to scare the evil spirits away at midnight. The following days of the New Year celebration are filled with visiting back and forth between extended family members who live locally, as well as neighbors, friends, and coworkers.

Growing Up the Chinese Way in the United States

How do American parents determine what "growing up the Chinese way" means? To American readers who tend to find it hard to define what is distinctively American, it may seem surprising to find that many Chinese have no such problem. There are differences in spoken language, food preference, and citizenship; however, these are secondary to the common cultural threads and Confucian philosophy that identifies one Chinese person to another and that defines hierarchical family relationships. Chinese parents, whether living overseas in Taiwan, the PRC, or Singapore, show surprising agreement about what it means to grow up the Chinese way (S. Lau, 1996). But, surely, growing up the Chinese way is different than growing up Chinese-American with adoptive parents who are not Chinese. What elements are these parents inclined to introduce into their American homes? What elements are they not inclined to introduce?

Adoptive parents take a typically American approach to bi-cultural socialization—picking and choosing what suits them! They ignore political holidays and many of the traditional Chinese values. Thus, they may celebrate the Chinese New Year (but not October First, the PRC National Day) and are critical of the hierarchical family structure, as well as the idea in traditional Chinese culture that men are superior to women.

Nor do most American parents want to instill other traditional Chinese values, such as modesty, not showing feelings in public, and deferring to parental judgements even in adulthood. These Chinese values are not the things that most American parents consider when they think about bi-cultural socialization. They are more likely to think in terms of forming personal relationships with Chinese people, learning the Chinese language, eating Chinese food, and becoming knowledgeable about Chinese traditions in the same way that other children have learned the traditions of their immigrant ancestors, for example, Irish-American Roman Catholics watching St. Patrick's Day parades and eating corned beef, or Polish-Americans attending local Kielbasa Festivals and dancing the polka. In the case of Chinese children, because they will be readily identifiable as Asian every day, the need for cultural identification and celebration may be even greater.

The purpose of bi-cultural socialization is not to teach American parents to emulate Chinese parents. Even if they want to, it is impossible for American parents to truly have their children "grow up the Chinese way" in the absence of a reinforcing culture in everyday life. (Even Chinese parents living in the United States find this to be a problem.) Instead, the purpose of bi-cultural socialization of adopted children is more limited. It tries to restore some of the positive things associated with the birth culture that these children left behind when they immigrated, which can provide them with a sense of their cultural roots. Even this more limited objective requires a substantial commitment of time, money, and effort.

FILLING IN THE CHILDREN'S BACKGROUNDS

At some point, it is likely that children adopted from China will ask questions about where in China they come from. Most will also visit the PRC, if not as children, then as adults, and want to see for themselves the province from which they came. Indeed 90 percent of the parents said it was either "somewhat" or "very" important that their children learn about the local areas of China that are their origin. What inferences can adoptive parents make about their children's backgrounds based on more general knowledge?

According to the 1990 Chinese census, the vast majority of the Chinese population (approximately 92 percent) is ethnically Han. There are also about 55 other ethnic groups constituting the other 8 percent of the population. These ethnic groups are called "minorities" in China, and most of them live in areas that border other countries. Because classification as a minority population is associated with a number of social welfare benefits, including being exempted from the one-child policy, it is very likely that the abandoned children are of the majority Han ethnicity (Soled, 1995).

In spite of the attempt, after the founding of the PRC, to make Mandarin the official language, there are still many regional dialects. These dialects have pronunciations, grammars, and vocabularies that differ from the official and formal Mandarin language taught in the schools. Some dialects have word usages and pronunciations so different that they might be considered separate languages in terms of speakers communicating with each other.

There are four major regional dialects spoken in China: *Bei-fang*, *Wuyue*, *Min*, and *Yue* (Cantonese is one type of *Yue*), and within each of these, there are even more different versions. To illustrate the differences within and across dialects, in the province of Guangdong a person might speak both Mandarin and Cantonese at work and *Tashan* (another dialect of *Yue*) at home. A person who speaks only Cantonese can barely understand a person speaking *Tashan*. In certain areas, there is an old Chinese saying that expresses this diversity: "Thirty *li* (almost 10 miles) away, you don't share the same traditions; fifty *li* (about 16 miles) away, you don't speak the same language."

The abandoned children most likely listened to (and perhaps learned in a small way to understand) the local dialect spoken by the caregivers in their orphanages or foster care situations. Most of the provinces from where the children were adopted, for the most part, use various versions of the *Beifang* (northern) dialect. These provinces are Hebei, Hunan, Anhui, Hubei, Sichuan, Shaanxi, Guizhou, Guangxi, Yunnan, and Jiangxi. Other children were adopted from provinces where, for the most part, the other three major dialects are used. The *Min* dialect is used mostly in Fujian Province, the *Yue* dialect is used mostly in Guangdong Province, and the *Wuyue* dialect is used mostly in Jiangsu and Zhejiang Provinces, as well as in the city of Shanghai.

The preparation of food varies across China. Contrary to the popular American belief that all Chinese people eat rice, some Chinese people prefer foods made from wheat flour. In the north, steamed bread (corn or wheat) and noodles are the most common staple food rather than rice.

Out of the four major schools of Chinese cooking, which have different theories behind the ways of preparing food, three apply to the provinces from where the children come. These schools are the Guangdong, the Sichuang, and the Huaiyang, and all prefer rice over noodles. The Guangdong (Cantonese) way of preparing dishes is well known for its roasting and stew-ing of all kinds of meat, including some that sound very un-usual to Americans, such as snakes, mice, and frogs. The Huaiyang school is one in which the original flavor of the food is more important. In contrast, the Sichuang school emphasizes seasonings and spices. Thus, the vast majority of the children come from provinces where rice is the traditional staple food, but the flavoring and preparation varies according to the local preferences.

The foregoing are just some of the inferences that can be made about the children's cultural biography. Adoptive parents also return from China with their own first-hand knowledge which they can later share with their children. Parental experiences in the PRC may also have stimulated them to think about what it means to grow up in China as compared with the United States. In the next chapter, we will learn that although many adoptive parents take an enthusiastic attitude toward Chinese socialization, others take a different approach based on the idea that their adoptive children are first and foremost Americans, albeit Chinese-Americans.

Chapter 5

PARENTAL ATTITUDES

As we have noted previously, adopting from China presents American parents with decisions about whether and in what ways to help their adopted children construct bi-cultural identities that include their birth culture. Some adoptive parents feel a strong obligation to provide their children with bi-cultural socialization and take an enthusiastic attitude toward having their children learn the Chinese language and celebrate Chinese holidays. Others strongly believe that their children are Americans first. Still others see value in stressing both Chinese and American socialization and struggle to find a balance.

In this chapter, we use both quantitative and qualitative data to describe various attitudes toward bi-cultural socialization. We asked the 526 study parents about their attitudes toward both Chinese and American cultures. In addition to the structured questions, the questionnaire provided the adoptive parents with the opportunity to express in their own words their ideas about bi-cultural socialization. Also included are discussions of parental perceptions of opportunities for Chinese socialization, and their reactions to applying for and receiving U.S. citizenship for their children. We begin with an overview of the different ways that the American parents conceptualized bi-cultural Chinese-American socialization.

AN OVERVIEW OF THE DIFFERENT APPROACHES TO BI-CULTURAL SOCIALIZATION

As their own words will show, the parents did not agree on how to approach bi-cultural socialization; their comments suggest that they emphasized one of four somewhat overlapping models. Three of these models roughly correspond to major categories that have been used to model patterns of immigrant adaptation in the United States to a second culture: *assimilation*, *acculturation*, and *alternation* (LaFromboise et al., 1993). A fourth model was also expressed that we call child choice. In this model, parents assume that their attempts at socialization can never be absolute and that their children should be active agents with respect to their own bi-cultural socialization, summarized in the expression—"she will choose for herself."

The first three models used to categorize the experiences of new immigrants presume that there are two (or more) clusters of ethnic characteristics (e.g., languages, values, and cultures) to which a child (or an adult) can be socialized. The construction of confident and effective social identities will depend on how conflicts between competing standards are resolved.

The argument underlying the *assimilation* model is that the standards of American culture are "privileged" and that a positive self-identity can best be achieved by fully accepting the perspectives of the dominant majority in the United States. The new immigrant is expected to lose his or her old cultural identity and fully accept a new one to be absorbed into the more desirable culture. Portes and Zhou (1994) have noted how the characteristics of recent immigrants have implications for their assimilation into American society:

> [T]he descendants of European immigrants who confronted the dilemmas of conflicting cultures were uniformly white. . . . Their skin color permitted them to skirt a major barrier into the American main-stream. As a result, the process of assimilation depended largely on the individual's decision to leave the immigrant culture behind and to embrace American ways. This advantage obviously does not exist for the black, Asian and mestizo children of today's immigrants. (pp. 19–20)

The argument underlying the *acculturation* model conjectures that the new immigrant will find it necessary to learn the new ways of the United States, but he or she also will retain some elements of his or her own culture. This model particularly applies when the new immigrant is a member of a visible minority that has not yet been fully accepted as an American. "[T]he acculturation model implies that the individual, while becoming a competent participant in the majority culture, will always be identified as a member of the minority culture" (LaFromboise et al., 1993, p. 246).

The premise underlying the *alternation* model is that it is possible for the immigrant to learn two different cultures well enough to be able to alternate between them as the context demands. It is speculated that "individuals who can alternate their behavior appropriately to two targeted cultures will be less anxious than a person who is assimilating or undergoing the process of acculturation" (LaFromboise et al., 1993, p. 250).

The theory of the psychological impact of bi-culturalism emphasizes both the risks as well as the benefits of bi-cultural socialization. The theory developed as a reaction to the notion that ethnic identities are always at risk when immigrants are faced with the need to become competent in a "second culture." Criteria for evaluating different models include knowledge of cultural beliefs and values, positive attitude toward both groups, bi-cultural efficacy, communication competency, role reper- toire, and groundedness (LaFromboise et al., 1993). In the case of children adopted from China, interestingly, parents face the need to educate their children in a "second culture" which they themselves do not share.

Child choice may represent a uniquely American parental re- sponse to the issue of bi-cultural socialization, one that is par- ticularly associated with the cohort of parents who came of age in the 1960s. These parents, recalling their own middle-class childhoods, may still feel antipathy toward the notion that older generations should force any choices on younger generations. Some parents also stressed the importance of providing early opportunities so that the child can make an informed choice when he or she gets older.

The next sections present parental comments that illustrate each of the four models. Although the comments indicate some overlap between the models (e.g., even parents who emphasize American socialization also want to instill pride in Chinese heri- tage), most parents clearly emphasized one model over the other. Where permission was given, we use direct quotes from their own responses to illustrate these models, and in other cases, we restate or paraphrase the substance of the comment. (We have slightly edited some statements to protect confidenti- ality and to improve readability.) Since the focus of this book is bi-cultural socialization, we begin with the approach that em- phasizes socialization to Chinese culture.

Acculturation: Focus on the Chinese

The first pattern emphasizes an energetic and enthusiastic ap- proach to the construction of a Chinese cultural identity for the child based on the belief that it is crucial that the child learn about her birth culture even though the parents are not themselves Chinese. Several parents described this approach as "immersion." One parent wrote of the Chinese activities that the family is now providing and of their future plans to nurture the child's birth culture: "We are making a strong effort to raise our child bi-culturally—with a Chinese baby-sitter during the week who speaks in Chinese and teaches Chinese characters. We think it is very important that our child be exposed to the best of Chinese culture while growing up and plan to visit China many times."

Where the family lives is also consequential as one mother pointed out in her comment: "We live in a wonderfully rich Chinese community. We are taking Chinese lessons together. She is registered to attend Chinese-American school when she starts kindergarten. We have wonderful Chinese friends, including a sweet 80-year-old-lady who calls her granddaughter and treats her as such. My daughter is very proud of being Chinese, something that has occurred as a result of the above."

This approach is sometimes associated with a preexisting interest in Chinese culture. Thus, another mother wrote of both parents' history of majoring in Chinese/East Asian studies, speaking Chinese, and having lived and traveled extensively in China and Asia. She noted, "Any child of ours (had we been able to have one ourselves, or an adopted child) would have been raised bilingually. I would like to send my child to an international school which is fully bilingual—pre-kindergarten through high school—so that she can become truly bilingual. I am working on organizing such a school within the next few years."

Others see bi-cultural socialization as a larger issue of *family* socialization. For example, "We see it as bi-cultural family socialization, not just for our child. We are a Chinese-American family now—more families need to see this fact! We have taken

Chinese middle names to demonstrate that as our daughter joined our family, we joined hers—other families could also consider this (and we're learning Mandarin as a family). It is worth moving religions, neighborhoods, towns, states, making new multi-ethnic friends, etc. to help your family become multi-cultural."

At other times, this approach is focused on what are perceived as obvious shortcomings in American society. This perspective is strongly expressed in the following comment: "This [the question of bi-cultural child socialization] is complex since I don't really feel very 'in sync' with mainstream USA culture, which is secular, consumption-oriented, violence-tolerant and homophobic. I think more about how important it is for my daughters to fit into a world with Chinese peers than I do about helping them fit into mainstream American culture. I hope they don't fit into mainstream American culture."

Assimilation: Focus on the American

The second approach focuses on socialization to American culture in order to enable the child to construct an American identity that transcends race and ethnicity. This model derives from the logic of *assimilation* in which immigrants are encouraged to quickly adopt the values and beliefs of their receiving country and to deemphasize the language and culture of their sending country.

This perspective finds strong expression in the words of an adoptive Chinese-American parent: "From observing my own Chinese family members, I find it ironic that many adoptive parents are more worried about inculcating Chinese culture than the Chinese are! Chinese-American families do require more discipline and more work from their children—I wonder whether American parents can really instill such values! I don't think our children should be raised 'bi-culturally'—this is not

China! Instill pride and understanding of Chinese culture, of course, but our children are now Americans first."

Another parent wrote, "There is a 100+ year history of Chinese immigrants to the US and I see our daughter as a part of that, with her own story. I want her to learn about how other Chinese people have come to and become part of America and to see herself as Chinese-American in that sense." Another parent also emphasized the hyphenated-American experience. "As a history teacher, I understand the problems that are created in our multi-cultural society. We will attempt to raise our child as an American of Asian heritage with an appreciation for all people."

One mother noted, "I am more concerned that my daughter now feels like a stranger here in the US than that she learns about Chinese language and culture—I guess the main reason I try to expose her to Chinese culture is to help her with her self-esteem and so that Chinese people don't think she's uneducated—she can't compete with first-generation Chinese people for cultural knowledge and yet I suspect others will compare her with them."

Another parent also used the context of assimilation. "As an Italian-American whose grandparents all came from Italy, I don't get hung up on bi-cultural, bi-lingual, etc. We are all Americans from somewhere else—we keep lots of Italian customs and we will incorporate Chinese customs—and we wear green on St. Paddy's Day. I tell my oldest daughter that people are like flowers—all different colors, shapes and sizes and together we make a beautiful garden."

Another mother wrote, "At 12 months, my daughter is too young to begin teaching much about the Chinese culture. My attitude is that she is first an American, in the same way other second and third generation children from other ethnic groups identify with the American culture more strongly than their parents' home culture. I want her to learn about and be proud of her Chinese origins but I won't try to duplicate the upbringing she would have received if she'd grown up in China."

Another parent saw bi-cultural socialization as a nonissue, "Really not that much of an issue in our multi-cultural/racial family/community—Questionnaire reflects researcher's preconception of a high degree of racial/cultural awareness—I'd like to think most adoptive parents are just normal Americans, proud of their multi-cultural roots, but not obsessing on them—I happen to be filling this out on July 4th."

Alternation: Try to Balance the Chinese and American

Other adoptive parents seek to find a balance between Chinese and American identities, and in so doing to raise children who will benefit from hyphenated ethnic identities. These parents believe that their children can be competent at least to some degree in two cultures and learn to feel pride in being both Chinese and American. The parents who take this approach often worry about how to find an appropriate balance or equilibrium. For example, a mother wrote, "I worry that we are giving enough of a balance. I want her to be proud of her Chinese roots but I don't want her to feel out of place. I cannot understand what it is like to be a racial minority in this country and I hope I can give her the tools to deal with the discrimination she will experience as she gets older."

Parents also pointed out that Chinese socialization can come at the expense of American socialization. One adoptive mother wrote: "I do not know what is the right amount of exposure to both worlds. I am worried that I will not be able to provide a real immersion in Chinese culture—I do not want her to be left out of the normal activities that help American kids gain confidence (like soccer on Saturdays), so I will not over commit her to Chinese events at the expense of her Americanization." Another parent acknowledged the importance of equally nurturing pride both in her daughter's birth culture and in her American heritage.

Another parent wrote, "Our major concern has been that our daughter concentrate on English improvement so she can keep up with other kindergartners in the fall! I do not want to confuse her with Chinese language classes yet—which is, anyway, very different from her own dialect. Our elementary school offers Chinese language daily, so when she is a bit older and her English adequate, we may start her with Chinese. (I don't believe that so-called languages classes once a week for 2-year-olds makes any sense.) Having been adopted at an older age, she needs more attention on typical American pre-school skills now, so she can happily achieve in school."

Another wrote, "My philosophy is to help her find her way, not to impose either rigorous Chinese training or a huge dose of the worst of American culture. There is much that is beautiful and good in each, but she must choose in the end. I think more about her day-to-day growing spirit and body and mind, than I do her ethnicity. For me, over concentration on her race and on Chinese culture can become its own ghettoization. So I try to find a good middle ground."

Another parent wrote, "While America is known as the 'melting pot' around the world, it is not (no longer) true that newcomers are melted into the American (largely Irish-English) culture. We find that our area is culturally diverse, as if it were an 'equal opportunity' (i.e., equal access) world. I wonder if obtaining or retaining a specific cultural (or even bi-cultural) identity is even possible. Our household is already a blended one."

Child Choice: Let the Child Choose

The final approach emphasizes the importance of the child's choice with respect to nurturing her Chinese identity. It may be discerned in the following comments. As one parent stated: "She is Chinese by birth, and Jewish-American by the country and parents who are raising her. As parents, we cannot dictate what part (cultural, religion, etc.) she will follow. All we can do is make her strong, self-reliant, and know right from wrong, and believe in herself. She will have to make her own choices."

Other adoptive parents noted the importance of early exposure to Chinese culture so that the child's choice would be grounded in experience. Thus a parent wrote, "We are lucky my child and I live in a city that is 60 percent Asian—most first and second generation. We shop at Asian markets, we go to festivals . . . my child is racially Chinese—she lives in America and adores Elmo—and she likes pandas, can show you where China is, can recite all the Chinese spoken in 'Big Bird goes to China.' But I am also aware that it is important for me to make sure she's comfortable as an American as well as a racially Chinese/American. Hope that makes sense. There is a lot of pressure from other FCC parents out here to pretty much 'define' their kids as 'Chinese.' "

Parents also pointed out that there is more to constructing an identity than just ethnicity. "My child is a lot of things, which Chinese is one. I'm going to take her lead on this and if she wants to know more about China, learn the language—I'll make that available for her—but I will not force her."

Another parent wrote, "Since my child will only know one culture I don't think Chinese values and attitudes will mean that much to her as a child in her everyday life. We plan on exposing her to Chinese culture and take her lead in what is of interest to her. By the way, we had no control over her liking Barney! She saw him at 9 months and has been in love ever since." In a similar vein another parent wrote, "I want our child to be an American with biological ties to China. She will be trained to be an American citizen. She will be told of her Chinese roots and given opportunities to learn about China as she desires. It will neither be denied to her nor pushed on her." And yet another wrote, "I want my child to learn as much about Chinese culture and her heritage as she thinks is important. I will support and encourage her, but if she is not interested, I will not push her. It is what is important to her that matters, not what is important to me."

Along the same vein, a mother wrote, "When she turns 3 she can go to Chinese school—I will give her that opportunity—give us that opportunity. As she matures it will be up to her how she wants to proceed. As an Asian Studies grad, I hope she wants to learn everything she can about China—being Chinese—and she's also an American kid and Elmo may win out—we'll see—she'll lead me."

Another parent worried that socialization to the Chinese culture might alienate children from their parents. "I plan to give her opportunities to learn about Chinese culture, but up to a certain point, since I myself am not Chinese, it will be up to her. Our area in California, of course, has lots of opportunities to learn about Chinese culture—including a Chinese (Mandarin) immersion school (pre-school to grade 12!!). My husband and I have not yet decided whether to send her there. We wonder whether sending her there will alienate her from us since we are not Chinese and trouble her that her mommy and daddy don't look Chinese like the other mommies and daddies."

Next, we turn from the qualitative illustrations of parental attitudes to our attempts to empirically measure attitudes toward Chinese and American socialization. We begin with an overview of the measures.

ATTITUDES TOWARD BI-CULTURAL SOCIALIZATION

We asked parents a series of thirty-two items designed to quantify their attitudes toward integrating Chinese values, language, and culture into the child's socialization. Each reflected some aspect of child socialization that might be reinforcing of Chinese identity. Richard Tessler and Gail Gamache developed these items in collaboration with Liming Liu, who has insider knowledge of the People's Republic of China. The items chosen emphasize parents' attitudes because parents will be making the choices for their children, at least during the early years.

In writing items for inclusion, we emphasized those things that Liming Liu believed would be important to a Chinese parent emphasizing traditional Chinese culture when raising a child. The vast majority of the items would be of obvious importance to a parent in China, such as language and cultural celebrations, as well as the values expected of a Chinese child. Some of the items dealing with values may also be important to Americans, such as studying hard, but others, such as not taking credit for individual achievement, are more distinctively Chinese. Chinese socialization includes teaching children to avoid taking credit in public for personal achievements and, more generally, that "modesty is a great virtue" (Hau and Salili, 1996, p. 132).

The purpose of asking American parents about these different facets of Chinese socialization was to find out what aspects of Chinese socialization were most important to them. In general, we tried to stay focused on culture (which we believed adoptive parents emphasize) rather than politics. Thus, for example, we did not ask parents about the importance of the National Day (October 1), which celebrates the founding of the PRC.

Since bi-cultural socialization implies connections to two cultures, we reasoned that it was also appropriate to measure attitudes toward American as well as Chinese socialization. Even though exposing children to aspects of American culture is less a matter of choice than is exposing them to Chinese culture, parents may still vary in the strength and content of their American attitudes, particularly with respect to popular culture. Thus, a somewhat parallel set of thirty-two items was developed by the researchers, drawing on their own histories as parents (and as a grandparent) to measure attitudes toward American socialization.

Several items were pointed out by Liming Liu to be distinctively American in that there is nothing comparable in China. Indeed, sleep-overs and celebrating Valentine's Day are particularly a problem for Chinese immigrant parents because they conflict with traditional Chinese values of privileging the family over peers and the total disinterest in Chinese culture of promoting romantic relationships between children. Celebration of Independence Day (July 4) and the Pledge of Allegiance were included because they are relevant to American citizenship, which all these children eventually obtain. (The PRC does not recognize dual citizenship.)

In the following sections, we turn first to the items focusing on parents' attitudes toward Chinese cultural socialization and then to parents' attitudes toward American cultural socialization (including socialization to U.S. citizenship).

Attitudes toward Chinese Socialization

Table 5.1 shows the level of importance ranging from "not at all important" to "very important" assigned to each of the thirty-two items of Chinese socialization by the adoptive American parents. For each item, such as the first, which was "learns to count in Chinese," the parent was asked: How important is it to you that your child (or children) have this as part of their experience growing up?

Overall, two observations from this table stand out. The first observation is that there is evidence that, regardless of the parents' overarching approach, there is at least some importance accorded to most of the measures of Chinese socialization. The second observation is that, with few exceptions, parents clearly do not all agree about the importance of specific facets of Chinese socialization. For example, parents are almost evenly split

Table 5.1
Responses to "How important is it to you that your child (or children)

	NOT AT ALL IMPORTANT	A LITTLE IMPORTANT	SOMEWHAT IMPORTANT	VERY IMPORTANT
learns to count in Chinese?	15.2%	22.1%	30.6%	32.1%
learns some Chinese words and phrases, such as, 'how are you?'	8.6%	16.7%	32.1%	42.6%
learns to write his or her name in Chinese?	11.4%	20.2%	29.5%	39.0%
becomes truly bilingual in English and Chinese?	35.0%	30.0%	22.4%	12.6%
is exposed to Chinese culture?	0.6%	3.4%	18.4%	77.6%
learns to eat with chopsticks?	28.7%	23.8%	22.1%	25.5%
likes Chinese food?	36.1%	23.0%	24.1%	16.7%
celebrate the Chinese New Year?	12.4%	20.0%	37.3%	30.4%
celebrates the Mid-Autumn Festival?	22.2%	29.5%	34.4%	13.9%
keeps his or her Chinese name?	29.3%	17.1%	21.5%	32.1%
listens to Chinese music?	28.0%	31.6%	28.3%	12.2%
listens to Chinese stories written to give a moral to Chinese children?	15.4%	26.6%	37.6%	20.3%
has an in-home child care provider who is Chinese?	76.2%	15.0%	6.5%	2.3%
becomes friends with other Chinese children?	4.2%	10.5%	29.3%	56.1%
has Chinese artifacts around the home?	5.7%	16.5%	32.1%	45.6%

118

Table 5.1 (continued)

	NOT AT ALL IMPORTANT	A LITTLE IMPORTANT	SOMEWHAT IMPORTANT	VERY IMPORTANT
learns about ancient Chinese history?	4.6%	19.0%	39.7%	36.7%
learns about modern Chinese history?	2.5%	13.1%	39.9%	44.5%
is able to communicate with you in Chinese?	63.9%	20.2%	10.3%	5.7%
visits China as a child?	48.3%	24.7%	13.9%	13.1%
visits China as a teen-ager?	12.7%	15.2%	38.0%	34.0%
visits China as an adult?	8.2%	9.3%	29.7%	52.9%
learns about the area of China from which he or she came?	1.1%	8.9%	32.7%	57.2%
visits a Chinatown in the United States?	16.0%	21.1%	28.5%	34.4%
watches Chinese movies or videos?	31.8%	29.1%	25.3%	13.9%
learns to appreciate classic Chinese poems?	26.8%	38.6%	26.1%	8.6%
learns about Chinese values and traditions?	3.2%	14.6%	39.4%	42.8%
learns the Chinese value of studying hard?	10.7%	17.7%	33.5%	38.2%
learns the Chinese value of modesty?	26.2%	31.0%	26.8%	16.0%
learns the Chinese value of the family as opposed to the individual?	16.5%	28.3%	33.3%	21.9%
is proud of his or her Chinese heritage?	0.6%	1.9%	8.4%	89.2%
learns to love his or her birth country?	7.4%	18.8%	29.5%	44.3%
is aware that he or she looks like other persons of Chinese descent?"	4.9%	7.4%	19.8%	67.9%

between the response categories when it comes to things like learning to eat with chopsticks and keeping the child's Chinese name. Although some parents feel that it is somewhat or very important that their child likes Chinese food, more than half feel that it is either not at all or just a little important.

Table 5.2 shows the six items (ranked by average scores) that were most important to parents. The items thought by parents to be least important (between "not at all important" and "a little important") are shown below the double line.

Table 5.2
Selected Attitudes Toward Chinese Socialization

How important is it to you that your child (or children):	Mean
is proud of his or her Chinese heritage?	3.86
is exposed to Chinese culture?	3.73
is aware that he or she looks like other persons of Chinese descent?	3.51
learns about the area of China from which he or she came?	3.46
becomes friends with other Chinese children?	3.37
learns about modern Chinese history?	3.26
visits China as a child?	1.92
is able to communicate with you in Chinese?	1.58
has an in-home child care provider who is Chinese?	1.92

Note: Response Categories are 1 = not at all important; 2 = a little important; 3 = somewhat important; 4 = very important.

Parents were especially likely to agree that it is very important that their child: is proud of his or her Chinese heritage, is exposed to Chinese culture, is aware that he or she looks like other persons of Chinese descent, learns about the area of China from which he or she came, becomes friends with other Chinese children, and learns about modern Chinese history. Among the items thought by parents to be least important (between not at all important and a little important) are: has an in-home child care provider who is Chinese, is able to communicate with you in Chinese, and visits China as a child. These last three socialization experiences are probably the most difficult to provide in terms of parental resources of money, effort, and time.

When the thirty-two items are used to construct a summary scale, the average score is 2.76, which is closer to "somewhat important" than to "a little important." When individual items are used in factor analysis, there is evidence of three factors that underlie parents' responses to the items: culture, values, and language. The highest factor score is obtained for the importance that parents attach to introducing their children to Chinese culture (mean = 2.89). The next highest score is obtained for the importance that parents attach to their children learning Chinese values (mean = 2.64). The lowest average score is related to the importance that parents attach to their children learning the Chinese language (mean = 2.51).

Opportunities for Chinese Socialization

Of course, parental desires may be also constrained by opportunities. Thus, we asked parents, "In general, how much opportunity do you currently have to provide opportunities for your child(ren) to learn about his or her Chinese heritage?" Less than 1 percent answered none at all. Some 15 percent answered a little. Slightly more than 50 percent answered some opportunities, but not as much as they wanted, and 33 percent replied that they had all the opportunities that they wanted or needed.

When offered the chance (in an open-ended question) to describe what additional opportunities they would like for their child (or children) to learn about his or her Chinese heritage, parents often responded by saying that they wished for more interaction with Chinese-speaking adults and families. One parent wrote, "I would like for our family to become friends with Chinese-American families—I would also like my child to know Chinese-American adults in all walks of life." Another parent noted, "I would like to meet ethnic Chinese in this country (not just adopted Chinese)."

Opportunities were often linked to the locale where the family lived such that one parent wrote, "living in an area that has a population base of 25 percent Asian, we have all the opportunity we need." Another wrote that "we are lucky to have a number of Chinese schools in our local community." Still another noted that "I am blessed to live in an area rich with opportunity." Still another wrote, "We live in New York City. If we can't find ample opportunity here, I don't know where else we could, outside of China itself." As expected, in local areas where there were few Chinese people, adoptive parents tended to report less opportunity for Chinese socialization. Thus, one parent wrote, "We have no Chinese friends and not many opportunities to meet Chinese people," and another parent wished for a "larger Chinese population in our area."

Several parents wrote extensive wish lists. One wrote, "I'd like to live somewhere with a large Chinese population. I'd like Chinese language classes in the public schools. I'd like the opportunity to have a Chinese nanny. I'd like to be able to visit China more often, and for my Chinese friends to visit us more often. I'd like culture camps close by. I'd like to know more about videos and written materials." Another commented, "I would like to have friends who are of Chinese heritage that my child could associate with. I would like her to be able to visit China and her foster parents many times. I would like to know something of her personal history and circumstances of her abandonment."

Other parents also found it difficult to form connections with ethnic Chinese people but did not mention the lack of local Chinese people as a constraint. The following are representative of these comments: "better access to Chinese adults," "more opportunities to play with (and talk with when she's older) other Chinese-American children and adults," and "more acquaintances of Chinese descent to help teach my child traditions and values." One parent noted her need to acquire expertise in using local resources, "We are ten miles from the University, which has a large Asian population. We only need to learn to use these resources." Also mentioned were "Chinese-speaking child care providers" and "a Chinese-speaking baby-sitter/mother's helper."

Chinese schools and language and culture classes were also mentioned as opportunities that would be taken advantage of in the future. One parent wrote, "when my child turns 3 she can go to Chinese school—I will give her that opportunity—give us that opportunity." But, another parent noted that some opportunities are constrained by eligibility criteria and wished for a "Chinese language school that begins earlier than the age of four." Parents also wished for particular programs such as "Chinese speaking school." Another wrote that "I would love it if when they enter school, they were enrolled in a Chinese immersion program." One parent saw her child's adolescence and young adulthood as the time of opportunity and wrote: "I expect that in junior high school and college, she will be interested in formal Asian/Chinese studies courses."

Moving from one area to another was mentioned as both a potential positive or negative event. Thus, one parent noted the lack of desired opportunities in her area and wrote, "I would love for our family to have Chinese families as friends so that our child can see other Chinese children with Chinese parents—I would love for her to be in a more ethnically mixed area (we are thinking of moving)." Another noted, "Last year we moved from an area where there was an abundance of Chinese programs and adopted children, to an area where my daughter is the only Asian adopted child in her class. I have searched for alternative sources and friends—[but] most have very young children."

Because of the young ages of many of the children, Chinese culture camps were an often mentioned opportunity in the future for both child and family. For example, one parent wrote, "We plan to attend a Chinese culture camp when she is older, and for her to study Chinese at a nearby school (also when she is a little older)," and another wrote, "The idea of a Chinese culture camp every summer for the whole family is very appealing." Another parent wanted "a Chinese culture camp [but] she is still very young—as she gets older, we will take advantage of the cultural camps and heritage clubs."

"More local festival celebrations would also be welcome—we would be willing to travel some for this, too." Also mentioned were "easier access to a Chinatown," "travel to China in the future," and one parent wished "to live in China, Taiwan, Hong Kong or Singapore." Parents also wished for educational resources for themselves such as "better access to media—books, movies" and for shows "that have Asian kids/people as primary cast (in English)."

Attitudes toward American Socialization

Based on the assumption, noted above, that bi-cultural socialization implies connections to two cultures, we also measured parents' attitudes toward American socialization. These items are shown in Table 5.3.

Table 5.3 shows the level of importance assigned to each item by the proportions of parents who responded in various ways. The results show that there is at least as much variation with respect to parental attitudes toward American socialization as there is toward Chinese socialization. This may reflect the growing importance of subcultures in the United States and the decline in shared Western values.

Table 5.3
Responses to "How important is it to you that your child (or children)

	NOT AT ALL IMPORTANT	A LITTLE IMPORTANT	SOMEWHAT IMPORTANT	VERY IMPORTANT
learns about *your* ethnicity?	9.9%	23.6%	35.0%	31.6%
celebrates holidays like the Fourth of July?	10.5%	14.8%	30.6%	44.1%
uses his or her American name?	9.5%	16.2%	31.8%	42.6%
learns a foreign language other than Chinese?	17.7%	22.8%	40.5%	19.0%
enjoys Western classical music?	26.8%	26.6%	30.0%	16.5%
goes to 'sleep overs' at a friend's house?	10.5%	12.0%	35.4%	42.2%
likes American food?	16.5%	23.0%	35.0%	25.5%
celebrates religious holidays such as Christmas and/or Chanuka?	8.0%	11.4%	24.0%	56.7%
celebrates Valentine's Day?	40.5%	25.1%	20.7%	13.7%
is proud of his or her American heritage?	4.0%	8.9%	28.0%	59.1%
sees Disney movies?	37.6%	29.1%	20.3%	12.9%
visits Washington, D.C. as a child?	33.7%	28.5%	24.7%	13.1%
becomes friends with children of many ethnicities?	0.0%	1.5%	13.1%	85.0%
joins groups like the Brownies or Cub Scouts?	21.9%	30.0%	29.7%	18.4%
watches *Sesame Street* or *Barney*?	27.6%	28.5%	26.8%	17.1%

Table 5.3 (continued)

	NOT AT ALL IMPORTANT	A LITTLE IMPORTANT	SOMEWHAT IMPORTANT	VERY IMPORTANT
has a Barbie doll or a Batman figure when his or her friends do?	57.4%	22.2%	13.9%	6.5%
learns about American history?	1.0%	4.4%	28.9%	66.2%
learns the Pledge of Allegiance?	15.2%	15.0%	28.1%	41.6%
visits Disneyland?	42.4%	26.4%	19.2%	12.0%
plays sports appropriate for his or her age?	5.9%	15.8%	39.2%	39.2%
learns your family history?	2.3%	12.4%	29.9%	55.5%
knows his or her extended family?	1.0%	2.7%	13.5%	83.1%
is exposed to Dr. Seuss books?	19.4%	27.6%	35.7%	17.3%
refers to your friends by their first names?	40.3%	28.5%	21.9%	9.3%
learns Mother Goose nursery rhymes?	23.6%	32.7%	30.8%	12.9%
learns about American values and traditions?	2.3%	9.1%	34.4%	54.2%
is popular at school?	12.9%	34.2%	43.9%	8.9%
learns the American attitude of valuing healthy self-esteem?	1.0%	5.3%	30.4%	63.3%
dresses like other American children?	13.9%	30.6%	39.5%	16.0%
forms close relationships with people outside of the family?	0.0%	3.4%	23.8%	72.4%
visits the Statue of Liberty?	38.6%	31.4%	20.7%	9.3%
learns to love his or her adopted country?"	3.0%	8.4%	26.3%	62.4%

Table 5.4 lists the items (ranked by means) about American socialization that were most and least important to the adoptive parents. We again use the double line to separate these two groups. To be included above the double line, an item would need to have an average response of between "somewhat important" and "very important." To be listed below the double line, an item would need to have an average response between "not at all important" and "a little important." Examination of the results shows that the most important future aims were that the child: become friends with children of many ethnicities, knows his or her extended family, forms close relationships with people outside of the family, learns about American history, and learns the American attitude of valuing healthy self-esteem. In contrast to the items on Chinese socialization, only one was seen on average as less than "a little important." This was having a Barbie doll or Batman figure when his or her friends do.

When the thirty-two items are used to construct a summary scale for American socialization, the scale has a mean score of 2.81, which is closer to "somewhat important" than to "a little

Table 5.4
Selected Attitudes Toward American Socialization

How important is it to you that your child (or children):	Mean
becomes friends with children of many ethnicities?	3.82
knows his or her extended family?	3.79
forms close relationships with people outside of the family?	3.68
learns about American history?	3.61
learns the American attitude of valuing healthy self-esteem?	3.56
has a Barbie doll or a Batman figure when his or her friends do?	1.69

Note: Response Categories are 1 = not at all important; 2 = a little important;
    3 = somewhat important; 4 = very important.

important" and is slightly higher than the mean score for Chinese socialization (2.76). (This is a statistically significant difference.) Factor analysis indicated three underlying factors: forming relationships outside the nuclear family, patriotism, and American popular culture.

Forming relationships outside the family rated 3.33 in importance, and is indicated by becoming friends with children of many ethnicities, playing sports, being popular at school, and forming close relationships with people outside of the family. *Patriotism*, also rated 3.33 in importance, is indicated by celebrating the Fourth of July, being proud of their American heritage, learning the Pledge of Allegiance, and learning to love their adopted country. *Popular culture*, which is concerned with helping the child to have the same experiences with popular culture as other American children, such as celebrating Valentine's Day, watching Disney movies, and visiting Disneyland, was rated lowest in importance (2.24).

In the next section, we attempt to identify social correlates of socialization attitudes using the summary scales rather than factor scores.

SOCIAL CORRELATES OF BI-CULTURAL ATTITUDES

Attitudes toward *both* American and Chinese socialization are generally positive and are significantly associated with each other, that is, if a parent scores higher on one he or she tends to also score higher on the other. In contrast, the area of the United States in which the family resides was unrelated to attitudes toward either Chinese or American socialization. However, the availability of opportunities for children to learn about their Chinese heritage was related to the area of the country in which the family lived. Parents on the West Coast, particularly California, reported significantly more opportunity for the children to learn about their Chinese heritage, or at least "as much as they wanted or needed."

There was a tendency for higher satisfaction with the China trip to be associated with more positive attitudes toward reinforcing the Chinese language, values, and culture. There was also a tendency for parents who visited the orphanage (for either a first or second adoption) to report more positive attitudes toward Chinese socialization (but not toward American socialization) compared with parents who did not visit the orphanage. Similarly, parents who were given the opportunity to keep in touch with their child(ren)'s caregivers (for either a first or second adoption) attached significantly more importance to Chinese socialization (but not to American socialization) compared with parents who were not given this opportunity.

Attitudes toward both American and Chinese socialization were unrelated to income, age, and religion. However, as years of schooling increase, positive attitudes toward American socialization significantly decrease. Parents who are currently married report somewhat less positive attitudes toward Chinese socialization when compared with parents who are not currently married. Parents whose children adopted from China have non-Chinese siblings reported slightly less positive attitudes toward Chinese socialization, and slightly more positive attitudes toward American socialization. Mothers and fathers differed on attitudes toward Chinese socialization, with women reporting slightly more positive attitudes. By contrast, there were no significant differences between mothers' and fathers' attitudes toward American socialization. Interestingly, the more parents reported being committed to the Chinese socialization of their children, the more they also reported negative social reactions toward their bi-cultural families.

Several reasons for adopting were significantly associated with attitudes toward Chinese and American socialization. Wanting to have a parenting experience, wanting to have someone to count on emotionally as the parent gets older, and wanting to pass on values to the next generation were associated with positive attitudes toward both. In addition, positive attitudes toward Chinese socialization were associated with not wanting to add to the world's population. Positive attitudes toward American socialization were associated with wanting someone to carry on the family name, wanting to have someone to take care of the parent as he or she gets older, wanting someone to fulfill unrealized dreams, and wanting to provide opportunities for a child that the parent did not have.

Also associated with positive attitudes toward Chinese socialization was membership in FCC. Members of FCC reported slightly more positive attitudes, but it is unclear whether FCC fosters more positive attitudes or whether people with more positive attitudes join FCC. Parents whose first choice was adopting in China also had more positive attitudes toward Chinese socialization than those for whom China was not the first choice.

RECEIVING AMERICAN CITIZENSHIP

On the assumption that parents would seek U.S. citizenship for their children, we asked what applying for and receiving citizenship meant to the parents. At the time of the study, 36 percent of the first adoptions and 50 percent of the second and third adoptions had already become American citizens. Applying for citizenship is a protracted bureaucratic process that cannot be initiated by the parents until the adoption is finalized in the United States. Thus, many parents tend to put off seeking citizenship during the period they are adjusting to their new parenthood. As is revealed in the comments written by those parents who had applied for and received citizenship for their children, many noted that receiving American citizenship was quite meaningful. Others reported annoyance with the bureaucratic process. Some parents reported that it represented a sense of closure and/or security, and others noted that it made traveling out of the United States a possibility.

The following are typical of the statements that included many of these reactions. One parent wrote, "Applying was a pain because I was sick to death of filling out forms. Her having citizenship is important because it is easier for us to travel together and it makes me feel more secure. For my child, I feel it is one more positive step in terms of her having a sense of 'belonging' and being an integral part of the culture." Another wrote, "Securing her place in this country—getting her an American passport for travel—securing her tie to us as a family." Still another wrote, "It provided some closure to the adoption process—could get an American passport to travel outside the US—made her feel more a part of our family—gave her the benefits of American citizenship—made her officially a Chinese-American, less risk of her being deported someday." Another wrote, "Mostly it put closure on the adoption process for me—it was the last step of the process—also I was surprised to feel happy for my daughter because it also meant that she now would reap the benefits of our great country with no repercussions." Still another wrote, "Final step in 'legitimizing' the process of adopting built family continuity (we're all American)—made me feel more secure to travel out of the US with her."

Some parents noted mixed reactions, including feelings both of relief and of loss. For example, one parent wrote, "A further 'reinforcement' that she was really 'ours'—a reminder that we took her away from her culture and her history and forced her into the American lifestyle." Another parent wrote that "I still have mixed feelings about changing my child's citizenship (and her legal name) without her understanding—on the one hand, of course, it makes us feel safer in our legal status with her, but I also feel that we've taken something away from her." And still another wrote, "I was not in a hurry to apply particularly because there was more money involved ($110 including photos)—I did so because there is a possibility we may return to China and I wanted my child to be a citizen and travel on an American passport—at the time of the citizenship hearing, I was conflicted about making such a monumental choice for my child." One parent expressed a more negative view: "Nothing, particularly—it's just a way to make a living in the US and [to make] dealing with the government a no-hassle affair for our daughter—I'm speaking in the future tense here because we have not yet applied for citizenship but will do so soon—I really don't care what nationality my daughter is."

But most parents emphasized what they considered the positive values of American citizenship, including rights, freedom, opportunities, and security. The following are representative of a much longer list of positive comments.

Citizenship for one parent meant "Protection for my daughter by being entitled to same rights as any citizen—eligible for US passport—same citizenship for parent and child." In the same vein, other parents wrote, "Our child would now be an official part of the United States and entitled to benefits (except being President) as any other citizen is." "The final step to her security and adoption completion, and most importantly the opportunities for her to grow up in America with all the opportunities, education, and freedom we wish for all people." "To me it means that her journey home is now complete and that she is entitled to all rights bestowed by our Constitution." "Made me feel secure that she would stay in the US if anything ever happened to me and she was orphaned. Also made me proud that she was an American citizen." "A sense of security that now they were citizens neither the Chinese nor American governments could deport them." "My daughter is entitled to all benefits/opportunities the US affords. She can't be taken from me by another government—another level of protection." "It meant our children were now safe and secure and would remain with us without worry of international politics." "It's important she adopt a new citizenship so she may have the prospect of freedom." Another two parents wrote, "Security, another milestone that made her mine," and "security, adoption completion, opportunities."

The following are typical of comments about the connection between citizenship and international travel: "She was free to travel with us to adopt her little sister," said one parent. Others wrote about "ease of international travel." "That our child could get a US passport and travel with us without restrictions." "It meant to me that she is safe to come and go in the world outside the US." "Getting a US passport so we could return to China to visit; safety in travel (no risks about visas, re-entry visas, etc)."

Several parents noted that the event was a special celebration. Said one, "It meant a lot to us. It was a very special day. It made us feel 'safer' that she was a legal US citizen especially with the anti-alien sentiment in the conservative faction in our society in control at the federal level of our government." Another parent wrote, "Her citizenship ceremony was held in a local elementary school that had made a school-wide project of the event—our daughter was among 22 children who became citizens in a touching ceremony that celebrated diversity. Our daughter's grandparents were on hand to join in the celebration." And another noted, "The idea of becoming an American citizen is not to be taken lightly and it [is] something we are delighted to share with our bio son and friends." Another parent wrote, "For me, citizenship was the most happy event after the adoption itself. I am very proud that my daughter is an American. I believe this is the greatest gift we have given her after becoming her parents."

Other parents linked gaining new citizenship with joining the new family. The following are representative of these views. "It made her even more just like the rest of the family and cemented one more thing we have in common." "It meant we would have US papers showing her to be our child." "She will be confirmed as one of us."

MORE THOUGHTS ON BI-CULTURAL SOCIALIZATION

International adoptions represent naturally occurring experiments that document the power of culture to socially construct identity. If, instead of being adopted by American parents, these children had remained in China, their Chinese socialization would be complete and their American socialization would be irrelevant. By contrast, if an American child were raised in China by Chinese adoptive parents, it is very unlikely that Chinese adoptive parents would be concerned about their child's American socialization. Indeed, personal communications with many overseas Chinese persons indicate much difficulty understanding what motivates American parents to attempt bi-cultural socialization.

The key to these cultural differences may lie in the fact that, unlike China, America is a heterogeneous society composed of many ethnicities and subcultures, each with its own customs, values, and beliefs, in contrast to China, which is far more homogeneous with respect to race and ethnicity. Most Americans accept that it is possible to be a true American at the same time that one is proud of one's ethnic origins. In the next chapter, we examine empirically through our questionnaires how much support exists for bi-cultural socialization in America and the early societal reactions to the American & Chinese families formed through international adoption.

Chapter 6

PUBLIC REACTIONS

On December 12, 1997, the Organization of Chinese Americans issued a press release that reported the results of a recent meeting between Asian Pacific Americans (APAs), President Clinton, and Vice President Gore (Organization of Chinese Americans, 1997). At this meeting, Daphne Kwok, executive director of the Organization of Chinese Americans, commented, "We urged the President and the Vice President to remain strong on emphasizing the contributions that Asian Pacific Americans have made in this country and that we are citizens just like everyone else." How far there is to go in achieving this goal can be inferred from the list of issues that were discussed at that meeting. Of major current concern to Asian-Americans was Bill Lann Lee's nomination for assistant attorney general for civil rights, but there were also long-standing concerns for access to health care, bilingual education, food stamps, immigration reform, elimination of sweatshops, and racial and economic justice more generally.

It is unlikely that the Chinese children adopted into comfort-able middle- and upper-class American families will face the prospects that poor Asian-Americans face, such as lack of health care or working in a sweatshop. But, affluence is no guarantee that this newest type of Chinese-Americans will be recognized as full Americans, when even Asian-Americans of Bill Lann Lee's stature face a "glass ceiling." Thus, adoptive parents of Chinese-American children who look different from the major-ity of Americans are understandably concerned with helping their children avoid the social marginality associated with mi-nority status at the same time that they seek to nurture their chil-dren's rich cultural heritage. It would be ironic if the search for bi-cultural identity reinforces the division between what is Chi-nese and what is American, and thus makes marginality more rather than less likely.

To put the issue of societal reactions into broad social con-text, we begin by examining the views of various groups toward adopting from China. We include the American media's view, the adoptive parents' published view, the Chinese view, and the Chinese-American view of these adoptions. We conclude with the real life experiences of the study parents. What reactions have these families encountered in American society? How much, if at all, have they found their adopted children to be tar-gets of racism? How much social support do these families re-ceive from people with whom they interact, that is, their relatives, friends, neighbors, child care providers, doctors, min-isters, and rabbis?

THE AMERICAN MEDIA'S VIEW

Media coverage of adoptions from China began to appear in 1992 in local and national newspapers, and has grown along with the adoptions themselves. By 1997, stories related to Chi-nese adoptions had also appeared in popular magazines such as the *Reader's Digest*, *Life Magazine*, *Woman's Day*, *McCall's*, and in less mainstream publications such as the *Yale-China Review*. There are several prointernational adoption themes that are prominent. One major theme is American parents rescuing abandoned Chinese babies from impoverished, understaffed, or horrific orphanages (Burkhalter, 1996; Smolowe, 1996; Eisenberg, 1997). The following scene described in the *Reader's Digest* is from a story told about an adoption worker's first visit to an orphanage in the PRC in August 1992.

> When Christian missionary friends told her about the grim conditions at the state orphanage in Nanning, across the border in China, Chan decided to see for herself. A hot morning sun beat down as she walked up a dirt path to the concrete building. Inside, she presented diapers and small gifts to the workers—good-will tokens that she hoped would make her unexpected visit acceptable. They did, and the director allowed her to explore at will. Chan was shocked by what she found. Rusty metal cots each held five babies, lying horizontally like swaddled sardines. Many of the babies had rashes and appeared malnourished. Others, glassy-eyed and motionless, lay oblivious to the flies hovering about them. Cries reverberated off the walls, yet no one was there to comfort the children. (J. M. Lau, 1998, pp. 98–98)

Even stories like this, which begin with descriptions of deprived babies, end on a heart-warming note with happy babies in loving American homes. As examples of triumph over adversity, they also serve the function of educating the general public about this new family form which they might encounter in the grocery store or at the mall. Such articles emphasize how much the adoption means to the parents and how quickly the children adjust to life in America. They are usually illustrated with photographs of "beautiful babies" or family scenes vividly conveying the parents' joy in their flourishing children.

Some of these articles also describe the efforts being made to educate the children about their roots (Loisel, 1996; Youtz, 1997; Scott, 1997). There are scenes of children in Chinese language classes, celebrating the Chinese New Year, enjoying Dragon Boat Races, and even playing hopscotch using Chinese characters on the family driveway while the parents look on proudly.

Although most American media coverage portrays adoptive parents in very positive ways, there are instances in which the motivations for adopting from China are implicitly called into question. Some glossy magazine coverage has treated the adoptions of Chinese babies as a chic and upper class fad on a par with owning a Mercedes or a Porsche ("Your Up-to-the-Minute Guide," 1997). Along these lines, *The New Yorker* published a cartoon equating interracial adoption to choosing between an Oriental or a Navaho rug. The cartoon depicts two white obviously middle-aged urban professional couples at a dinner party. The caption reads, "We're so excited. I'm hoping for a Chinese girl, but Peter's heart is set on a Native American boy" (Hamilton, 1997).

American media coverage is also quite critical of China's role in the adoptions. Often this is more apparent in the title or subtitle than in the text, where, for example, an editorial decision is made to refer to an otherwise positive article entitled "I Met My Daughter at the Wuhan Foundling Hospital" on the magazine cover as "China's Market in Orphan Girls" (Porter, 1993). There are also individual stories of adoption trips gone awry, and of disturbing incidents in other countries where international adoptions have had unhappy outcomes (L. Smith, 1995). Still others focus on these adoptions as a symptom of what is wrong with China—its preference for boys, its one-child policy, the conditions of its orphanages, and its alleged human rights violations (Thurston, 1996). In 1996, a special Internet site focused on the "Dying Rooms" controversy. That year a report appeared that alleged that thousands of children had died in Chinese orphanages from "starvation, medical malpractice and abuse" (Burkhalter, 1996; Tyler, 1996).

THE ADOPTIVE PARENTS' VIEW

In contrast, the community of adoptive parents has taken a different position based on their *personal* experiences in China, arguing that most orphanage conditions were far better than what was described in the media coverage of the "Dying Rooms." This argument presumes that their personal exposure to information about the plight of abandoned Chinese children was representative, which may be a dubious assumption in a totalitarian country that is able to enforce a one-child policy, mandate abortions and sterilizations, and threaten political dissidents. It is not that American adoptive parents are unaware of the human rights controversy connected to China. Instead, they choose to focus on the positive elements of Chinese culture rather than on politics (Youtz, 1997).

Indeed, one can see the philosophy of focusing on the positive elements of Chinese culture in the FCC Internet site, the FCC-sponsored list serves, and the various newsletters. For example, the premier issue of *The Red Thread*, a quarterly magazine devoted to articles about the adoptive families of Chinese children, explains the name of its magazine in the following way: "Red is a very important color in Asian cultures. It symbolizes good luck. In the Chinese culture, one of the beliefs is that a 'red thread of life links all Chinese people together. The 'red thread' is now commonly being used to describe and symbolize the love and link of adopted children with their families" (Brown, 1998, p. 1).

In stating their belief that the red thread ties all Chinese people together, the editors imply that the adoptive parents are coming to think of their families, if not themselves, as Chinese. In fact, in going to cultural events, taking language classes, and using chopsticks at home, many parents have adopted not only Chinese children but Chinese culture as their own. Still, for many of these bi-cultural families whose primary link with China is through adoption, the cultural connection is artificially constructed. This is not to suggest that the benefits of such efforts are insubstantial, but only to differentiate it from the bi-cultural socialization that the children of Chinese-American parents may receive.

In her book *Are Those Kids Yours? American Families with Children Adopted from Other Countries*, Register (1991) provides a cogent rationale for efforts to provide bi-cultural socialization for adopted children, be they Korean, Latin American, or Chinese:

> We who have adopted children with no memories have the responsibility of constructing a past that incorporates both personal data and cultural knowledge. It can be constructed deliberately, with special care to make it livable—a past that causes no shame or lasting regret, even if it has elements of tragedy, or it can be a clumsy structure, made of the scrap lumber of ill-considered comments and assumptions made in ignorance. (p. 127)

However, Youtz (1997) suggests that the explicit effort to adopt not just the children but also the culture may be mainly an urban and professional response:

Not every adoptive family seeks out Chinese culture activities, of course, although it is striking how many do. In contrast to the model of the urban, professional parent or parents, is another large group of adoptive families coming from smaller towns across the country, frequently with a strong Christian orientation. Although it is very difficult to generalize, I sense that many of these families place greater emphasis on seamlessly mixing Chinese adoptive children into the American melting pot, with fewer opportunities and less enthusiasm for surrounding them with the culture from which they came. (p. 11)

Whether or not they are pursuing bi-cultural socialization, many adoptive parents are joining groups such as FCC. Founded in 1993 by a small group of adoptive parents in New York City's wealthy and educated upper west side, FCC expanded rapidly, and by 1997 included over eighty chapters in North America (Scott, 1997). The larger chapters were publishing newsletters; sponsoring support groups, cultural events, and language classes; and encouraging charitable contributions to Chinese orphanages. The emergence of FCC reflects the belief that families with children from China need to support one another.

FCC also has a homepage on the Internet and sponsors two list servers, one for prospective parents and another for post-adoptive parents. Both positive and negative responses are salient in the messages posted. One can read everything from comments about the offensiveness of *Sesame Street* having a male worm-puppet named Slimy competing in a diving contest against a Chinese female worm-puppet named Lo Mein, to informed discussions about why children under six months of age are generally not available for adoption in the PRC.

THE CHINESE VIEW

Chinese scholars and government officials concerned with international adoption express the humanistic view that the adoptions are helping to foster greater understanding between the United States and PRC. As an expression of this interest, two professors from Anhui province, Banghan Huang (professor at Anhui Agricultural University) and Liyao Wang (research associate, Anhui Academy of Social Science), came to Amherst, Massachusetts, in the winter of 1996 to interview adoptive parents. Professor Huang Banghan wrote a brief article for a FCC-sponsored newsletter after being in the United States for three months and interviewing fifty families in New England and New York City. (Professors Huang and Wang subsequently interviewed an additional forty-eight families, including some in Florida.) Since this is one of the few pieces of information that we have about how the Chinese view the adoptions, we quote liberally from it.

> When I left for the U.S., my relatives, friends, and the directors and staff of several children's welfare institutes in Anhui all said the same thing. "You must go visit the adoptive families personally to see how the girls adopted by Americans are living now." I understood that all of them were concerned about the adoptees' fate with some suspicions. "I will, I must," I told them. "That is the main purpose for my visit. I will speak the truth." (B. H. Huang, 1998, p. 1)

Professor Huang saw his task as one of explaining why American parents adopt Chinese girls, and putting to rest some suspicions that some Chinese people have about international adoption.

People in China often ask me why those Lao Wai
(meaning foreigners) come here to adopt their children. Why don't they give birth themselves? Why
don't they adopt in America? Is it possible that they
bring these girls abroad for drug-testing (to be
guinea pigs in experimental drug-testing)—like the
Japanese did in its war of aggression in China during
World War II? Is it possible that they will raise these
girls for servants or arranged marriages or even pros-
titutes? Do these Lao Wai without children know
how to take care of the babies? These suspicions
showed that many Chinese people just don't understand why Americans adopt children from China.
(B. H. Huang, 1998, p. 3)

After returning to the PRC, Professor Huang's co-
investigator responded to these suspicions in a two-part article
in one of the provincial newspapers of Anhui entitled "Lao Wai
Adopt Chinese Babies" (Wang, 1997a, 1997b). In addition to
seeking to explain to Chinese readers the reasons that Americans
adopt babies from China, he described the positive outcomes of
the adoptions he encountered in ninety-eight adoptive families:
"These adopted babies are very happy in their American families. Almost all children have their own bedrooms and a separate
space set aside for play. Their parents are very busy with doing
various things for them happily. This really reminds one of the
proverb 'What sacrifices parents under the heaven have to make
for their children' " (Wang, 1997a, p. 15).

In applying the Chinese proverb, Professor Wang implies that
these Chinese children were receiving no less care and devotion
from their American parents than Chinese parents provide their
children. This is another way of saying that any negative suspicions of parental motives are unfounded.

Adoptive parents themselves report no such suspicions concerning their motives from the Chinese people they meet on the
street and in hotels in the PRC. When American adoptive parents, in the company of their children, encounter Chinese people in China, the response is almost uniformly positive. It is
summarized by the statement "She is so lucky" (Youtz, 1997,
p. 7). Anecdotal accounts suggest that many Chinese interpret
international adoptions as "good deeds by kind persons" (*hao
ren hao shi*) and that they believe that adoptive American parents
are very altruistic. An article in a major national PRC press recounted the story of a single American father who adopted a
handicapped Chinese girl. The impression given was how lucky
this girl was to have the opportunity to be raised in America
where she could receive medical attention for her handicap
(Cheng, 1997).

THE CHINESE-AMERICAN VIEW

The Chinese-American view of the adoptions is the least
known, even though it is potentially a very important one. How
Chinese-Americans view the adoptions may be linked to how
Chinese-Americans view themselves and their place in U.S. society. As Vivia Chen, a Taiwan-born Chinese-American who is
also an adoptive parent, observes, even the acceptance of the
term "Chinese-American" within the Chinese community has
changed over time.

> To my parents, . . . the term "Chinese-American" . . .
> applied to the descendants of Cantonese laborers
> who immigrated to America several generations ago.
> Chinese-Americans meant the people who filled the
> tenements and factories of the Chinatowns in New
> York and San Francisco, whose children (though
> American-born) spoke English with a Chinese accent

and continued to slave away in stifling laundries, cheap restaurants and dreary stores. [In contrast] the Chinese of my parents' circle came to this country [from Taiwan] in the '50s and '60s for graduate studies (usually in fields like math or science) and never perceived themselves to be "Chinese-American." They referred to themselves as "Chinese." At the same time, however, they were earnest Americans. My father, for one, took pride in owning a house in the suburbs, always paid his taxes on time and diligently voted at every election (almost always Republican). Like many of his generation and class, his identity was Chinese, but his sense of citizenship was American. . . . Today, being Chinese-American has a different connotation. The new generation of American-born Chinese readily calls itself Chinese-American. (Chen, 1997, p. 2)

It would appear, therefore, that there have existed divisions within the Chinese-American community that were based on social class related to status differences that arose in China. More recent Chinese immigrants are accorded higher social status than earlier immigrants. The Chinese experience is the mirror opposite of other ethnic groups, where the earlier one's ancestors arrived in the United States, the more status the current generation has (for example, the Daughters of the American Revolution).

Thus, the Chinese-American view of the adoptions may be confounded by social class. Chinese-American adults who grew up in immigrant families in Chinatown, and who continue to struggle even to make ends meet, may doubt the sincerity of bicultural child socialization because to them it suggests personal advantage rather than a real interest in the welfare of the Chinese-American community. If the interest was sincere, they may argue, it would not have had to wait for the adoptions to take place.

Other Chinese-Americans who immigrated years ago and have worked hard to be accepted in American society may resent FCC's orientation to the PRC rather than to the Chinese-American community. Some of these immigrants chose not to encourage their children to learn to speak or write Chinese, and in this sense have less knowledge of Chinese culture to share. This may be why some adoptive parents believe that the more acculturated Chinese-Americans will have less knowledge to offer about Chinese culture.

The segment of the Chinese-American community that appears to be most receptive to and interested in the adopted children and their families are second- and third-generation Chinese-American professionals and scholars who are themselves rediscovering pride in their Chinese roots. But even these persons are more concerned, and understandably so, in working to achieve economic equality, full participation in the political process, and social justice for all Chinese-Americans than in joining with adoptive parents in celebration of a shared Chinese heritage.

REAL-LIFE PROBLEMS

What societal attitudes get communicated in real-life situations was one of the research questions underlying our study. Instances of insensitive questions and comments containing racial innuendos are often cited on the Internet and occasionally in FCC newsletters. But how widespread and representative are such experiences? Is it mainly the negative experiences that are given voice, though the vast majority of adoptive families experience more positive societal responses, or is there in fact a social stigma associated with adopting from China? Here research asking systematically about family experiences would seem to be able to best address the issue.

In our survey, we asked the study parents how much of a problem negative reactions had been in a variety of social situations. The areas were the neighborhood, the child care setting, the supermarket, restaurants, when traveling, comments from children, and extended family situations. Of the 500 parents who responded to this series of questions, most (56 percent) reported "no problem at all" in any of these 7 areas. About 18 percent reported at least some problem in 1 area, 9 percent in 2 areas, 12 percent in 3 or 4 areas, and only 5 percent in 5 to 7 areas (see Table 6.1).

When parents report problems, they tend not to report problems across many areas (median = 2 areas for those reporting at least one problem area), nor are they likely to report that it was

Table 6.1
Negative Reactions: Situations Rank-Ordered by Proportions and Means from Most Problems to Fewest Problems

Social Situation	Not at All %	A Little, Somewhat, or Very Much (%)	Mean
comments from children	75.0	25.0	1.30
in the supermarket	79.0	21.0	1.26
when traveling	82.0	18.0	1.22
at extended family occasions	84.0	16.0	1.20
in restaurants	85.0	15.0	1.18
in the neighborhood	92.0	8.0	1.09
in the child care setting	98.0	2.0	1.02

Note: Response Categories: 1 = not at all a problem; 2 = a little problem; 3 = somewhat a problem; 4 = very much a problem.

"very much a problem." Still, the existence of even minor problems is of concern to these adoptive parents. They are most likely to report problems arising from comments from children (25 percent), in supermarkets (21 percent), when traveling (18 percent), in social occasions that involved extended family members (16 percent), and in restaurants (15 percent). Only 8 percent reported that there was a problem in their neighborhoods. Negative reactions were almost nonexistent in child care settings (2 percent). A number of parents also expressed concern about whether social responses will continue to be positive when the children get older or when they are not in the company of their parents.

Real-Life Examples

There was also evidence of negative social interactions in response to an open-ended question that asked, "What reaction(s) from *strangers* has troubled you the most?" In response, 61 percent expressed various complaints, ranging from the annoying to the serious. Because of the visibility of these adoptions, these parents tend to receive questions and comments that other new parents do not face. Parents disliked what they perceived as "nosey" interest in international adoptions, that is, strangers asking intrusive questions.

Parents particularly resented it when these comments took the form of inappropriate questions asked in the presence of their children, such as "How much did she cost?" and "Why didn't her mother want her?" or of slighting remarks about China such as "China hates girls." Some parents were unhappy with the often-heard comment, "She's like a China doll," though others interpreted the remarks as welcoming and kindly meant. Some mothers reported being asked, "Is her father Chinese?" and some parents reported a Chinese caregiver being mistaken for the child's mother. These families are also subjected to many comments that have to do with adoption in general, such as the attitude that adoption is a second best way to create a family.

Rarely were overtly racist comments reported, but when they did occur they were unsettling. One parent recounted a story of "an adult man in a fast food restaurant with his wife and daughter pointing to my daughter and calling her a 'chink baby' (his wife punched him in the shoulder)." Another parent noted that the reaction that troubled her the most came from her ex-boss. "She said that I never had to worry about my daughter being smart because she probably came from peasant stock and all they do is dig in the dirt." Another parent said, "Once I was incensed when an elderly man referred to my daughter as a 'half-breed' (since I am Caucasian, he assumed my husband was Chinese)."

Other such comments seemed to derive from U.S. military history with a few veterans holding grudges against Asian peoples even when they are unable to differentiate among Japanese, Korean, Vietnamese, and Chinese peoples. One parent noted receiving verbal "comments from veterans of the Korean war who feel it necessary to tell me how awful Oriental people are." The same parent also reported the comment "couldn't get a white one, huh?" Another parent reported receiving "stares (hostile) from men who, I hypothesize, served in Vietnam." Another parent reported, "a Vietnam vet who told my baby he had 'killed a lot of your cousins.' "

One parent noted that U.S. military history may also affect the attitudes of family members. She noted, "Strangers, oddly, have been no problem . . . My father was the big problem. Fifty years ago, he was shooting at the Chinese in Korea. He's not 100 percent comfortable with my daughter even yet." Another parent anticipated these reactions and observed, "One other issue was critical in selecting China—family members who served in the military never fought against Chinese people, but along side them. We never want our children to have been the enemy of living relatives."

It is not just Caucasian-Americans who sometimes react negatively. One parent noted, "Oddly, the reactions that may be considered negative have come from Asian strangers' 'double takes' on the street or in a Chinese restaurant when the waitress asked how much she cost us." Another parent commented, "We get some chilling stares from local Native American Utes and Navajos who assume she is Native American. We just come right out and tell them she's Chinese and then they smile and are warm towards us."

SOURCES OF SOCIAL SUPPORT

We conclude with the potential sources of support for adoptive families. In the survey, we asked about a variety of potential sources of social support in dealing with issues of bi-cultural socialization. Parents were asked: "Overall, how supportive have each of the following been to you in dealing with issues of bi-cultural identity?" The sources were participation in FCC, pediatricians/health practitioners, extended family, friendships with other adoptive families with Chinese children, Chinese-American friends, neighbors, Chinese friends, minister, priest, or rabbi, American friends, and child care providers. The sources are also shown in the first column of Table 6.2. Columns 2, 3, and 4 show the distribution of responses for parents who had a particular source available. The far right-hand column shows the *number* of parents who did not have a particular source of potential support available, such as having a minister, priest, or rabbi, as opposed to parents who have the potential source available but report that it is not at all supportive.

Perhaps what is most striking about these results is *how much* actual support was received by the parents, according to their own reports. Parents reported from 0 to 10 sources of social support that ranged from "a little" to "very supportive." Only 4 parents (out of 526) reported no actual support from any of the

Table 6.2
Sources of Social Support: Ranked by Proportions Reporting
Very Supportive

Source: How supportive has each of the following been...	Very (%)	A Little or Somewhat (%)	Not at All (%)	Do Not Have Source (n)
friendships with other adoptive families with Chinese children?	79.84	19.96	0.19	10
child care providers?	61.96	33.25	4.78	108
Chinese friends?	61.94	33.22	4.84	216
Chinese-American friends?	60.59	36.20	3.22	153
American friends?	60.58	36.70	2.72	11
participation in Families with Children from China?	59.28	40.24	0.48	111
extended family?	58.30	37.26	4.44	8
minister, priest or rabbi?	47.22	39.23	13.54	238
neighbors?	42.41	48.65	8.94	45
pediatrician or health practitioner?	36.10	50.83	13.07	44

10 sources. On average, parents reported receiving support from between 7 and 8 sources (mean = 7.76). Over 15 percent received some degree of support from all 10 sources.

In general, informal sources were experienced to be somewhat more supportive than formal sources with the exception of child care providers. Opposition by family or friends was rarely mentioned. To the contrary, both family and friends (Chinese, Chinese-American, and American) ranked very high in terms of "very supportive." The most support was received from friendships with other adoptive families with Chinese children; this is not one and the same with (formal) participation in FCC which ranked lower. One parent commented as follows: "Although we live in an area of the country that has a reputation for bigotry, we have heard only positive comments and encountered smiles. We have several other friends in our city with adopted Chinese girls. We have made commitments to each other to have our girls frequently play together. It is important to us that they be friends as they grow up. They have much in common."

Favorable media coverage may also have been a factor in mobilizing support particularly from grandparents: "I think that the children who are being adopted now from China have a much easier time of it because of the press they have received. Both of my daughter's grandmothers were skeptical until the 'news magazine' shows started doing stories. If anything, she is treated as more precious and special."

With respect to friends, an alternative interpretation is that people who are not supportive are no longer friends. "It seems easier to socialize with our new FCC friends and other adoptive parents than some (not all) of our long-time friends. Our friends either understand why her culture is important or just don't have a clue. There seems to be little in between. I feel much closer to people who have either looked into adoption or adopted themselves. I sense a gap between my old friends who have biological children and our family."

Interestingly, in contrast to child care providers who were considered "very supportive," the least supportive source was pediatricians (and other health practitioners). Referring to one medical encounter in America, a parent wrote, "My daughter had an allergic reaction and had to go to the hospital emergency room. The nurse asked 'Is she yours or is she just adopted.' The doctor said he hated working on adopted kids because there is no family history."

About 13 percent of the parents rated pediatricians and other health practitioners as not at all supportive. Much of this dissatisfaction may arise out of the pediatricians' inexperience with caring for children adopted internationally. This is not to say that providers are not supplying quality health care, but rather to suggest that some pediatricians are uncomfortable in interactions with bi-cultural families.

Three fourths of the parents reported having Chinese friends and/or Chinese-American friends. Nonetheless, their comments suggest that they would welcome opportunities to expand their networks of both groups. The probability of having Chinese or Chinese-American friends varied significantly by geographic area of the United States. Ninety-five percent of the parents living in California had such friends compared with only 69 percent in the Midwestern states.

CONCLUSION

In some important respects, the brief experience to date of families with children adopted from China parallels the much longer experience of families who have adopted children from Korea. In his review of the literature on societal reaction to families with children adopted transracially, Silverman concluded, "Racial hostility seems to have been a very minor element in the lives of Korean adoptees and their families. None of [the] studies reported serious . . . opposition of family and friends, or frequent encounters with racial hostility" (1993, p. 108). On the other hand, more recent articles about Korean adoptees coming of age suggest that, as teenagers and young adults, they feel a need to return to their roots. The societal response to their search is plainly positive, as they are being encouraged by parents, adoption agencies, and each other to explore their past (T. Hong, 1997).

As noted in chapter 1, we expected that the societal response to the current wave of Chinese adoptions would be influenced by the history of Chinese immigration to the United States. As we have seen, this history appears to have different effects on how the adoptions are viewed by different groups. Many Chinese-Americans who immigrated some years ago and have struggled to fit into American society may well believe they have little in common with adoptive girls who "have fallen into a honey jar." Adoptive parents also appear to be distancing themselves from the image of the earlier immigrants from southern China who historically were less educated and did not speak Mandarin.

While the general response to these most recent immigrants is welcoming, the very fact that families with children adopted from China feel that they need continued support (as evidenced by membership in FCC) is itself an indication that these families view themselves as being outside the mainstream. Even as most parents experience full acceptance by family and friends, they are sensitive to comments from strangers, and they worry about how their child will be accepted at the playground, in the school, and beyond. Perhaps full acceptance will come only when nobody reacts in a questioning way to these families.

Chapter 7

LOOKING TO THE FUTURE

It should already be clear that bi-cultural socialization can take place for many families, as well as for the society more generally. Just as individual parents struggle with decisions about Chinese versus American identity, so too will the nation as a whole continue to struggle with a whole range of diversity issues during the twenty-first century. The need to respect social and cultural differences while also affirming commonalities is already a major source of social activism in America. Organized efforts to nurture subgroup differences while gaining acceptance within the mainstream of society will continue to be made by many groups who, like Families with Children from China, are concerned about appreciating distinctiveness while decreasing marginality. The highly educated and articulate parents who make up FCC appear poised to join in this struggle.

Regardless of the approach parents take to bi-cultural socialization, it is reasonable to expect that the children adopted from China will feel strongly about both their American and Chinese identities. Virtually all will be taught to be proud of their Chinese heritage, whether they learn the language or observe cultural holidays, at the same time that they internalize American culture and values. In most respects, they will be indistinguishable from other American girls in valuing individual autonomy, in how they spend their time, and in how they think about themselves. They will identify with their American peers, play soccer on Saturday, watch American television, and eat pizza and drink Coca-Cola. Even those who learn to speak Chinese, draw Chinese characters, eat with chopsticks, celebrate major Chinese holidays, and become knowledgeable about Chinese history and culture will have primary self-identifications as American.

So far the American reaction to these still young children, as individuals and as a group, appears to have been very welcoming. However, there is a long-standing tendency for many Americans to "habitually think of Asian Americans as 'foreign'" (Sumida, 1993). Thus, whether they will be accepted as "real Americans" as they grow up remains to be seen. The history of Chinese immigration to the United States indicates that we should not presume that societal reactions will always be welcoming.

Nor should it be presumed that the information the children receive about China will be uniformly positive. It seems likely that sooner or later the children will be confronted with negative information about China, whether on television, at school, or in conversations, to which they may need or want to respond. The challenge for parents is how to encourage pride in things that are Chinese without romanticizing and idealizing the birth country. Helping these children to have pride in their Chinese heritage goes well beyond individual decisions about whether to expose the child to Chinese culture, language, and values, and current political relations between the United States and the PRC. It also requires social changes premised on the belief that America needs to become more inclusive of Eastern culture and more accepting of Asian-Americans.

In this regard, it is encouraging to see the debate about having Asian-American studies programs as well as Asian programs in American universities. Calling attention to the need for such education, a graduate student in the English Department issued a challenge to the University of Massachusetts, asking:

> Does anyone know why Asians from China . . . came and are still coming to America? Do you know about their lives, their experiences as railroad workers, farm laborers, picture brides, refugees, and immigrants? Do you know how much they have contributed to the economic wealth and superpower of this nation? Isn't it about time you did know? Don't you think you have a right to know? (Ha, 1997)

Clearly, children adopted from China will also have a right to know, and should know, without having to wait for a college education. Education appreciating diversity needs to be incorporated in elementary and middle-school curricula.

BEING CHINESE-AMERICAN

Chinese-Americans (and other Asian-Americans) have an ambiguous status in the United States (M. Hong, 1993). Their status as a "model minority" has been positive for them at the same time that it has meant that their problems tend to be ignored, from the "glass ceiling" that affects middle-class Asian-Americans, to the cuts in social programs that affect poor recent immigrants. Although poor mental health outcomes tend to be more associated with class (poverty) than with race, lowered self-esteem is a possible adverse effect of racial discrimination even for children raised in affluent households.

Although the children at adoption tend to be developmentally lagged with respect to gross motor skills, parents report that they quickly catch up. They also learn English quickly, adapt easily to American foods, and readily accept their new families as their own. Rapid adaptation to American ways also has its "down side" with respect to Chinese socialization as aspects of popular culture may come into conflict with parents' efforts to nurture Chinese identity. The potential for conflict and arguments will increase as the child turns six or seven, makes her own friends, is exposed to their toys (e.g., a blond-haired Barbie rather than an unobtainable Asian "Michelle Kwan" doll), voices her own restaurant preferences (e.g., McDonald's rather than a Chinese restaurant), chooses Brownies over Chinese language class, and finds more "magic" in Halloween than in the mid–Autumn Festival.

The outcomes of the bi-cultural child socialization that has been the subject of this book lie in the future. Many parents remain convinced that over the long term providing bi-cultural socialization will give their children a way to cope with societal reactions that threaten to marginalize them, either by refusing to accept them as Americans or denigrating them as Chinese. Whether parents' attitudes will change, or be translated into practices, and whether this will make a difference ultimately to the children are all matters for follow-up studies. In terms of identity development, these children may be most similar to third- and fourth-generation Chinese-Americans, whose grandparents were the children of immigrants, and who have become Americans in language, culture, and values.

For those American parents who put a high premium on Chinese socialization, there are some cautions in writings by Chinese-Americans about growing up Asian-American. A major point of caution is that not everyone has the ability to become bi-culturally competent. Pardee Lowe, who grew up in San Francisco, graduated from Stanford University, and later received an MBA from Harvard, described his own attempt to become bi-culturally competent:

Unlike my American education, my Chinese one was not crowned with success. It was not that I was entirely unwilling to learn, but simply that my brain was not ambidextrous. Whenever I stood with my back to the teacher, my lips attempted to recite correctly in poetical prose Chinese history, geography or ethics, while my inner spirit was wrestling victoriously with the details of the Battle of Bunker Hill, Custer's Last Stand, or the tussle between the *Monitor* and *Merrimac*. . . . When it became apparent to [my tutor] that in spite of my extra hour a day, I was unable to balance cultural waters on both my shoulders . . . he informed me bitterly [that no amount of chastising] would ever unravel the cultural chop suey I was making of my studies. (Lowe, 1993, p. 185)

Adoption outcomes will not be limited to the influence of bi-cultural socialization. Another important influence is likely to be how the child comes to terms with her adoption history and the socio-political context in which it is embedded.

EXPLAINING ADOPTION HISTORIES

In most cases, by the time their child is three years old, parents will have already succeeded in presenting the fact of adoption to their children. Such explanations are, of course, a result of the obvious physical differences between parent and child. But explaining the larger "socio-political matrices of individual decisions" in terms that children can understand still looms ahead (Riley, 1997). As we look to the near future, another crucial issue for parents will be how to explain the circumstances of their children's abandonments to them.

These particular adoption experiences are occurring during a period of American social history where open adoptions and contact with birth mothers are becoming more normative. But parents who adopt from the PRC have little or no knowledge about their children's birth parents to share with their children. Paradoxically, this is also a reason why many parents chose China in the first place. However, their children (like all adopted children) are bound to show some curiosity about their birth parents, particularly in adolescence when they will struggle with questions like "who am I" and "where did I come from."

When parents were asked to comment on bi-cultural socialization, many expressed the difficulties they foresaw in having to explain China's one-child policy and the preference for boys that led to their children being available for adoption. Many parents suggested that their most difficult task might not occur until their children are older. One mother stated, "A key piece of my daughter's identity is that she is an adoptee from China. I think families need to really focus on the adoption piece—how to explain it, what happened, and why, in a political and social context that she can understand. The adoption piece is part of her bi-cultural identity. If we focus on the bi-cultural issues without grounding children in the adoption piece we will have seriously missed the boat and created much anxiety for the children."

As further indication of the scope of the dilemma, one parent commented, "I hope our daughter comes to grips with her adoption and it comes to cause as little anguish as possible down the road for her." Another said, "I hope that as she grows she will be able to travel and learn enough to understand the political and social realities that have led to the abandonment of so many baby girls in China. I expect that the issue of abandonment will be most difficult to come to terms with." Another commented, "I feel that our daughter's critical point in her life will be when she begins to conceptualize adoption, skin color, and the presence of birth parents in China whom she will never be able to identify."

Because explaining these adoptions goes beyond individual stories to larger socio-political and economic issues, these parents have little guidance as to what and when to tell. Other than a book intended for children entitled *When You Were Born in China: A Memory Book for Children Adopted from China*, no one has addressed the issue of adoption messages that parents who have adopted from the PRC will present to their children (Dorow, 1997). Eventually parents will need to explain to their Chinese-American daughters why being female was a major reason they were abandoned. This may conflict with the positive portrait that the parents have encouraged them to have about their birth country, since their daughters will view the Chinese preference for male children as something that devalues them as females.

The need to provide their children with explanations of why they were abandoned by their birth parents may be the first time that adoptive parents will realize that bi-cultural socialization includes politics as well as culture. It is possible that children who are strongly grounded in Chinese language, values, and culture will find it particularly difficult to accept the adoption messages that they receive about the circumstances of their adoption. The more positively these children come to feel about their birth country, the more difficult it may be for them to also accept that it was the one-child policy of the PRC and the cultural valuing of sons over daughters that led to their abandonments.

It also seems likely that entry into the social world of the school will raise questions about adoption. As the children enter kindergarten and then first grade, and as they gain some understanding of their background, a central issue will be whether achieving some level of bi-cultural competence has made it easier or harder for them to accept their histories. Although this may not come to a head until later, it seems likely that the questioning process will begin when children start formal schooling and come under the inquisitive glances of their peers. It is likely that other children will ask them why their mothers and fathers are not also Chinese, if only out of natural curiosity.

Imagine bringing your five-year-old to kindergarten, and while you are busy unloading coat, hat, boots, and backpack into her cubby, you are approached by a girl, perhaps a second grader, who asks if you are your child's father. When you reply in the affirmative, she responds by asking "Who born her?" You explain that your daughter was born in China and that you have adopted her. To your considerable relief, the girl says "That's cool!" and goes off happily to her own classroom. All of this occurs in front of your daughter. Although you are satisfied, more or less, with how you responded to this girl, you worry that the next time it may be an older child whose questions are even more pointed and who is not so easily satisfied. Also, since you no longer have total knowledge of the interactions in your child's life, at some point the questions may be addressed directly to her, and she will need to respond for and about herself. You can no longer protect your daughter from intrusive and possibly upsetting questions.

IMPLICATIONS OF THE AGE GAP

In looking toward the future, another point of concern is (or should be) the age gap between the parents and their children from China. Although some adoptive parents are drawn to China precisely because the PRC allows older parents to adopt, the fact that they are older, and often much older than typical "first-time" parents, suggests that their parenting experiences will be "off time" in terms of the conventional family life cycle.

At the time they completed the questionnaire, the median age of the fathers was 45 years (range = 30 to 73) and the median age of the mothers was 42 years (range = 27 to 52), and their children from China averaged 2 years of age. If we add 16 years in order to allow the 2-year-olds to graduate from high school, it follows that more than half their fathers will then be 60 or older, and more than half their mothers will be 58 or older. On average there will be about a 40-year difference between parent(s) and child. Although the legal obligation to support a child ends at 18 years of age, for these middle- and upper-class parents the anticipated years of dependency related to college and postgraduate education will continue the child's need for support.

Even a parent of a 2-year-old does not have to go so far into the future to recognize that a 40-year difference will pose problems for both parties. The present discussion is not intended to threaten these older parents but rather to help them anticipate the potential problems that they may face down the parenting road. Thus, the reader is advised to consider what follows as "worst case scenarios." As we will see, the issue of the age gap is both related to and independent of bi-cultural socialization.

In examining the stages in the family life cycle, we will return to the convention of asking the readers to imagine themselves as parents of children adopted from China. Accordingly, we address the reader in the second person as "you." The use of the second person is also intended to reinforce the speculative nature of this section.

Beginning in grade school, age stereotypes will increasingly become the basis for social comparisons. Whether at the school open house, the first PTA meeting, a school picnic, or other school-sponsored event, the age gap between you and your child will be conspicuous. The social ambiguity resulting from the off timedness of parenting young children will raise further questions about your relationship to the child. Now it is not just race but also age that draws attention to your nontraditional family. Other children may ask, "Who is that with [your child]?" Younger parents in their later twenties or early thirties may also be confused ("he's too old to be *her father*!") and feel awkward about approaching you. This awkwardness may even extend to your relationship with your child's classroom teachers. At some point, your child may become embarrassed by the age gap. The fact that older adoptive parents are not alone in experiencing the stigma of off-timed parenthood is of little consolation to you.

As the adorable five-year-old grows into an awkward, fresh eight- or nine-year-old, the age gap will be increasingly experienced as a generation gap. Like other children of this age, the peer group will become a more important influence in virtually every area of life, from how to dress, what television programs to watch, who to hang out with, and to what time to go to bed. Thus, you will begin to experience a loss of control which will naturally increase through your child's teenage years as pressure to conform to their friends' values rather than to yours intensifies.

Conformity to peer pressure will challenge both your own and your child's commitments to bi-cultural socialization. At the same time that you face decreasing energy levels, your child's capacity to fill the hours of your days will continue to increase. Coping with the ordinary tasks of parenthood such as chauffeuring your child to soccer games, swimming meets, and music lessons, as well as preparing their meals and supervising their homework, will seem to require the emotional and physical energy of a thirty-year-old rather than a fifty-year-old. Clearly you will have less energy left over for bi-cultural socialization, especially when your child resists.

You will be focused on the obligations of parenthood at the same time that other persons your own age will be skiing on weekends, playing golf or tennis, going to concerts, and planning foreign travel. During this middle childhood stage, you may look enviously at your own peers who, because they have already launched their children into adulthood, have much more personal freedom and increased resources to spend on themselves.

As your child moves into puberty, at twelve or thirteen years of age (recall that girls tend to begin puberty earlier than boys), it will be not only your daughter who is experiencing troubling and possibly disruptive mood swings. If you are her mother, and are now in your late forties or early fifties, you may be going through the hormonal changes associated with menopause. If puberty and menopause have independent effects on the mother-daughter relationship, what are the joint effects likely to be? How will the emotional and behavioral manifestations of these two hormonal changes be understood (or misunderstood) within the family?

To negotiate your child's teenage years, it is important that you continue to exercise influence. But will these sixteen-year-old girls pay as much attention to their older fathers' and mothers' advice and admonitions as they would if there was not a forty-year age gap? As a member of a generation that once believed that "you can never trust anyone over thirty," you now find yourself at the opposite end of the generation gap. It would seem that the age gap can only fuel adolescent rebellions as the older parents look to uphold their own traditions and values while their children (like all adolescents) embrace change. Thus, in your late fifties when your daughter no longer depends on you for transportation, and instead drives herself or gets rides from her peers, you may look back nostalgically on those days when you always knew where she was. As the parent of an adolescent, you may also have to get used to a whole parade of young people walking through, eating, and sleeping in your house. Thus, you may also look back nostalgically to those days when your permission was sought about who could come into your home and when.

If you are the father, your daughter will be setting off for college, perhaps to a school with hefty tuition and fees, around the time that you are turning sixty. In one sense, your age should be an advantage, at least financially, since your occupational earnings are likely to have peaked. But, in another sense, being sixty will be a disadvantage financially since college tuition and fees will compete with your own need to save for retirement and may produce reduced income in retirement. Your felt obligation to pay for your daughter's higher education may also encourage you to postpone retirement.

As your child reaches young adulthood, she will develop her own social network apart from the network of friends and family who support *your* position on bi-cultural socialization. She will develop her own attitude toward continuing her Chinese socialization, which may or may not be one with which you agree. She may either lose interest in Chinese culture or, by contrast, turn toward it. An important influence may be her future spouse and in-laws.

Assume your daughter has graduated from college and found a good job and that your "work" is complete somewhere in your mid sixties. Enter your future son-in-law who will bring a whole new set of dynamics to the family system. Will he be Chinese-American or (as seems more likely) Caucasian? Will his family be comfortable with your daughter's "Chinese-ness" or with your lack of "Chinese-ness"? Will they be concerned about your daughter's lack of information pertinent to family and genetic history? Will your much younger in-laws be comfortable with you? Indeed, the wedding pictures of the bride and groom in the company of both sets of in-laws may have what appears to be a three-generational quality, where you and your spouse appear to be grandparents.

Actual grandparent-hood, should you live to experience it, also will have an "off-time" quality, as you will likely be in your seventies before this role transition is experienced. If your daughter marries a Caucasian man, an important issue will be the intergenerational transmission of Chinese culture. What will be the preferences of your daughter and her husband with respect to passing on Chinese language, values, and culture to their children? Will they want to socialize your grandchildren bi-culturally? Whether your daughter chooses to socialize your grandchildren bi-culturally will likely depend on many factors, including the outcome of her own bi-cultural socialization.

From your daughter's perspective, one of the most important issues will be whether the age gap between her and you will deprive her of a healthy or living parent when she is still a young adult, or when she has young children of her own. With a forty-year age gap, she could be in her early thirties, raising her own son(s) or daughter(s), just as you are experiencing serious health problems in your seventies. This will leave your daughter (who will likely be an only child) in the difficult position of having to care for you at the same time that she has to care for her own children.

FCC AS A GROWING SOCIAL MOVEMENT

As already discussed in chapter 3, the formation of FCC represents the beginning of a social movement to make Chinese (and other Asian) Americans more accepted as Americans. It also represents an organized effort to build a cultural bridge between the United States and China, and to provide opportunities for children adopted from China to appreciate their ethnicity in the same way that most other Americans take for granted.

The growth of FCC is truly startling. Beginning with a handful of parents in New York City, there are now approximately fifteen hundred members in the greater New York area. In 1997, FCC had chapters in forty-three states and the District of Columbia. Many states included more than one chapter. Not surprisingly, the New York chapter has continued to take a leading role on the East Coast.

In letters to its membership, dated January 12, 1998, the FCC–NY Board of Directors summarized their accomplishments in the following terms:

For an all-volunteer organization, FCC has a great deal to be proud of. By joining together we have made a difference. We have created a network of support that helps others discover the road to China. That helps our children now, and will continue to do so in the years to come. And, that helps us all as parents. . . . We all share something in common and we did something about it. (Families with Children from China: Greater New York, 1998)

There is an interesting triple meaning in "the road to China." In one respect, FCC has clearly informed prospective adoptive parents of the process of adopting in China. In another respect, FCC is helping adoptive parents to continue on the cultural road to China so that bi-cultural socialization is a possibility. In addition, it is helping other Americans to appreciate the two-way traffic on the road that lies between the West and the East, and in that way is making Asian culture more accessible and desirable. The same letter recounts FCC–New York's organizational accomplishments, as follows:

FCC accomplished a lot in 1997: Our first comprehensive directory. Four more issues of our extraordinary newsletter. Our first fundraising effort, raising nearly $60,000 for orphanage programs in China. Another festive Chinese Culture Day. A full slate of captivating parent programs. Our stimulating adoption information sessions. Outreach efforts with the Chinese Consulate and Chinese cultural institutions. Numerous craft and holiday events. The list goes on. None of it would have happened without your support and the tireless efforts of many volunteers. (Families with Children from China: Greater New York, 1998)

FCC–New York was not alone in its philanthropic work in support of orphanage programs in China. FCC–New England has its own Foundation for Chinese Orphanages whose Red Envelope Campaign raised $41,000 in 1997. In letters dated January 16, 1998, the FCC–NE president informed the donors that this money is being used "directly to improve the lives of 2,000 of the more than 100,000 orphans still living in China" (Foundation for Chinese Orphanages, 1998).

Challenges Ahead for FCC

As with any social movement, there are bound to be disagreements. In the case of FCC, the disagreements tend to focus on whether bi-cultural child socialization is needed to reach the larger goals of producing individuals with positive self-identities and reducing the marginalization of Chinese-Americans. There exists, even among FCC members, a multiplicity of approaches, ranging from parents who believe that Chinese socialization is vital to their child's development, to others who do not believe that it is necessary or realistic to emphasize Chinese socialization. The differences of opinion suggest that FCC needs to be as inclusive as possible.

There is a real danger that some parents with children from China, who are not "into" bi-cultural socialization, will be intimidated by vocal and articulate advocates stressing extensive Chinese socialization. In addition, undue emphasis on bi-cultural socialization may have the negative, if unintended, consequence of creating divisions among the children, such that the very group that should serve as a primary support network will be divided among themselves in terms of who is and who is not being exposed to Chinese language and culture. Thus, one challenge for FCC is to encourage relationships between the children regardless of parental attitudes and practices with respect to bi-cultural socialization.

Having noted that parents do not all agree, we also want to express our surprise in finding that most of the parents who completed the questionnaire indicated that *Chinese socialization* held some degree of importance. For example, we had not known that American parents even knew about the mid–Autumn Festival, much less that 78 percent attached some degree of importance to celebrating it. For these mostly new parents, who are still in the process of bonding with their children, and particularly for those who have only recently returned from China, the questions that were posed in the study may have seemed abstract. Indeed, a fair number commented on this.

Even when new parents are truly committed to bi-cultural child socialization, translating that enthusiasm into consistent practice is likely to be problematic, especially if opportunities are limited. As children grow older, participation in Chinese cultural activities is going to face competition from other activities. For example, during the winter holiday season parents may have to decide whether to let their children attend a performance of the *Nutcracker Suite* or to insist that they attend the final meeting of a FCC-sponsored Chinese language class. During the spring, organized sports may compete with FCC monthly meetings in which parents and children form primary relationships.

Part of the key to supporting parents' efforts to help their child stay culturally connected to China may lie in creating opportunities for Chinese socialization which are embedded in normal life and routine. This may involve much ingenuity on the part of both parents and teachers. Although bi-cultural socialization may appear to be serious and didactic (and it is), it is important that exposure to Chinese socialization be as natural as possible.

We were also surprised that parents who completed the questionnaire accorded as much importance to *American socialization* as they did. The reader may recall from chapter 5 that responses appeared to indicate three underlying factors: forming relationships outside the nuclear family (e.g., making friends, being popular at school), patriotism (e.g., celebrating the Fourth of July, learning the Pledge of Allegiance), and exposing the children to American popular culture (e.g., watching Disney movies, reading Dr. Seuss books). In fact, American socialization (median = 2.81) scored slightly higher than Chinese socialization (median = 2.78) in terms of the importance accorded to each. Perhaps, as adults, these "children of the 60s" sense that for their adopted children American socialization is even more important than it was for them.

The challenges ahead are not limited to the children's connection with China, but will also include their connection to the United States, which lies more outside their individual control. Recall Julia Ming Gale's problem finding her cultural footing as a Chinese-American. "The thing I most resent [she said] is the loss of culture." Here Dick Lehr notes she is not talking about Chinese culture, but about American culture. "The fact [is] that I can't really claim the culture I grew up in, because people will never really let me" (Lehr, 1996).

For Ms. Gale, physical appearance is probably more important as a distinguishing characteristic than Chinese culture. From this point of view, others also see race rather than ethnicity as the main barrier to the acceptance of Chinese-Americans.

> Racial groups . . . may also have distinctive cultural traditions, as we can readily see in the many Chinatowns throughout the United States. For racial groups, however, their physical distinctiveness and not their cultural differences generally prove to be the barrier to acceptance by the host society. For example, Chinese Americans who are faithful Protestants and know the names of all the members of the Baseball Hall of Fame may well be bearers of American

culture, but they are still a minority, because they are
seen as physically different. (Schaefer, 1993, pp. 8–9)

Indeed, this view was confirmed in a newspaper article by a
Chinese-American college student at the University of Massachusetts about the problems she has had "finding a place in
America." She lamented that, even though she "was born in the
U.S. and grew up with *Sesame Street, Mister Rogers' Neighborhood*, the Babysitter's Club book series, and a lot of Coca-Cola,"
many Americans still consider her to be a foreigner or at least not
a real American. As a teenager, she traveled to Hong Kong with
her mother, and although she looked like everybody else, she
was considered different from the Chinese. Her relatives told
her it was the way she walked, the way she talked, and the way
she carried herself that identified her as an American. She reflects, "It's funny how I [had] to travel thousands of miles to be
considered an American" (Chan, 1997). Thus, explaining an
Asian physical appearance and an American manner is not just an
issue for children who are adopted.

Such personal narratives illustrate that many Chinese-
Americans feel that other Americans do not accept the American
part of their bi-cultural identity. Whether this is a reflection of
the same kind of xenophobia shown to earlier generations of
Chinese immigrants, or whether it rests on a different basis, is
really beside the point from the standpoint of adoptive parents.
Parents feel that they need to prepare their children for negative
reactions to their Asian-ness, whatever the source.

So where does this leave groups like FCC? Perhaps what it
does is challenge the movement to take a new look at what it
means to become an American from the perspective of the children, for whom being accepted as American will be so very important. Much work needs to be done to reinforce the concept
of America as a nation that includes Asians as real Americans.

Besides working to change public attitudes, FCC needs to do more to nurture a relationship with the Chinese-American community. When in our survey we asked who parents received support from in terms of becoming a bi-cultural family, it was surprising to us that less than two thirds of those who had Chinese or Chinese-American friends reported that they were "very supportive" in dealing with issues of bi-cultural identity. Chinese-Americans would seem to be their children's logical reference group. There are many obvious commonalities. Chinese-Americans look Chinese. Many, if not most, were raised in the United States and are American citizens. It would seem that Chinese-Americans have a much better idea of the problems that children adopted from China will face, as the statements of the college student quoted above illustrate.

Like most new mothers and fathers, the parents who participated in the study are coping with the demands of parenthood. Perhaps FCC can help families invent their futures by educating them about milestones in child development *before* they occur. Some of the children have already begun kindergarten and first grade, and other parents can learn from their experiences. The transition to formal schooling raises many important questions about how the children will be accepted, what kind of curriculum they will be exposed to, who will be their role models, and more generally about the loss of parental control that will be inevitable.

The leadership of FCC rightly takes much pride in its friendship with the PRC, and in its contributions to Chinese orphanages. However, FCC needs to be more than just a friend of China and Chinese orphans. It also needs to become an influential voice in helping Americans to appreciate their own history of immigration. As a nation of immigrants, many Americans need to be reminded to celebrate what makes them distinctive as well as what makes them one. Thus, as individual parents advocate for their own child, so, too, they will need to fight for the celebration of diversity more generally. FCC parents have the potential to positively affect the educational system's response wherever there are children whose culture differs from the majority culture.

THE FUTURE

At present, children adopted from China constitute a relatively small population in America, that may or may not continue to grow at the 1997 rate of approximately thirty-five hundred children per year. Much is at stake in the future rate of growth of this special population, including the clout that FCC will have as a social movement if enrollments drop or level off rather than continuing to increase. At a more psychological level, increases or decreases in new adoptions will also affect the risk of the children feeling alone and different.

Many factors will determine the future of adoptions from China, including changes in the one-child policy in the PRC, tension between the United States and China for whatever reasons, and, finally, incidents that embarrass or anger the Chinese government and cause it to slow down or end the adoption of Chinese children by *Lao Wai*. Interruptions in foreign adoptions can also happen unpredictably and without explanation, as the Chinese moratorium on adoption of 1993 demonstrated. Entire international adoption programs can be put in jeopardy by criticism from outside the country as was the case in South Korea, or by internal criticism, which was the case in Russia (Osborne, 1997).

Whatever the future rate of growth in adoptions from the PRC, the social significance of American & Chinese families may be far larger than their numbers. Efforts by many adoptive parents to make Chinese culture visible for their children in their everyday lives will also make Chinese culture more accessible to other Americans. In addition, the travels of American adoptive parents to China, especially in small to middle sized cities where most adoptions occur, will make Americans more visible and understandable in the PRC. In these ways, the formation of bi-cultural American & Chinese families has the potential for contributing to greater understanding between the United States and the PRC.

Many Americans are having their first central relationships with Chinese immigrants through their associations with children adopted from China. Aunts, uncles, grandparents, other extended family members, and friends are learning to like, to love, and to form attachments with this special group of Chinese immigrants. In addition, neighbors, coworkers, teachers, child care providers, doctors, and religious leaders, who might ordinarily not come in contact with recent immigrants, are learning that their own society is at the same time more global and less parochial than they might once have believed.

Americans who have adopted children from China have opened a very important door, one that is intensely personal at the same time that it is also social and political. Although no one can be certain what lies ahead, American & Chinese families symbolize an important meeting of West and East, which could not have been imagined in the political climate of the 1950s and 1960s. In their readiness to meet their children halfway around the world, the adoptive parents have taken some significant steps in demonstrating that humanitarianism is important regardless of nationality.

As America moves into the twenty-first century, we will see increasing dialogue between West and East in which the United States and the PRC will undertake to learn from each other, and to appreciate what each has to offer the other in more than just economic terms. American parents and their Chinese children are part of this dialogue, and are living examples of the real potential for improving understanding and goodwill. It will be very interesting to see if the larger social and political entities can live up to the examples being set by these American & Chinese families in their everyday lives.

BIBLIOGRAPHY

Abraham, W. 1995. "Imperial China—Origins to 1911." In *China: A Nation in Transition*, edited by D. E. Soled. Washington, D.C.: Congressional Quarterly Inc., 3–37.

Bachrach, C. A., K. A. London, and P. L. Maza. 1991, August. "On the Path to Adoption: Adoption Seeking in the United States." *Journal of Marriage and the Family* 53: 75–718.

Bian, J. 1996. "Parental Monetary Investments in Children: A Focus on China." *Journal of Family and Economic Issues* 17(1): 113–139.

Brown, K. A. 1998, Winter. "Untitled Quotation." In *The Red Thread: A New Quarterly Magazine Connecting the Adoptive Families of Chinese Children*, 1.

Burkhalter, H. 1996, January 11. "China's Horrific Adoption Mills." *New York Times*, section A, 25.

Chan, L. 1997, December 2. "Finding a Place in America." *Massachusetts Daily Collegian*. Amherst: University of Massachusetts, 5.

Chen, V. 1997, Summer. "Chinese versus Chinese-American." *Families with Children from China—New York's Newsletter*. New York: Families with Children from China, 1–2.

Cheng, X. 1997, November 22. "Love Has No Boundary." Shanghai *Jiefang Daily*, 8.

Chin, Ai-Li. 1978. "Being Chinese-American: The Reshaping of Identity and Relationships of One Generation." In *The Mixing of Peoples: Problems of Identity and Ethnicity*, edited by R.I. Rotberg. Stamford, CT: Greylock, Inc., 131–150.

"China Calls a Halt to Adoptions by Foreigners."1993, May 2. *Boston Sunday Globe*, 5.

DeBerry, K. M., S. Scarr, and R. Weinberg. 1996. "Family Racial Socialization and Ecological Competence: Longitudinal Assessments of African-American Transracial Adoptees." *Child Development* 67: 2375–2399.

Dorow, S. 1997. *When You Were Born in China: A Memory Book for Children Adopted from China*. St. Paul, MN: Yeong & Yeong Book Company.

Eisenberg, H. 1997, June. "Made in China, Loved in America." *McCall's*, 66–67.

Elliott, K. S., M. di Minno, D. Lam, and A. Mei Tu. 1996. "Working with Chinese Families in the Context of Dementia." In *Ethnicity and the Dementias*, edited by G. Yeo and D. Gallagher-Thompson. Bristol, PA: Taylor & Francis, 89–108.

Faison, S. 1997, August 17. "Chinese Happily Break the 'One Child' Rule." *New York Times*, section A, 1,10.

Families with Children from China: Greater New York. January 12, 1998. Letter to the Membership.

Fong, R. and I. Gusukuma. 1998, March 4–8. *From Policy to Practice: The Adoption of Chinese Children by U.S. Families*. Paper presented at the Council on Social Work Education, Orlando, Florida.

Foundation for Chinese Orphanages. January 16, 1998. "Report to Donors—Red Envelope Campaign 1997." Families with Children from China: New England.

Gordon, M. M. 1964. *Assimilation in American Life: The Role of Race, Religion, and National Origins*. New York: Oxford University Press.

Groza, V. 1997. "Adoption: International." In *Encyclopedia of Social Work* (1997 Supplement), edited by R. L. Edwards, I. C.

Colby, A. Garcia, R. G. McRoy, and L. Videka-Sherman. Washington, DC: NASW Press, 1–4.

Groze, V. and D. Ileana. 1996. "A Follow-up Study of Adopted Children from Romania." *Child and Adolescent Social Work Journal* 13(6): 541–565.

Ha, N. 1997, December 9. "Looking into the 21st Century: The Need for Asian-American Studies." *Massachusetts Daily Collegian*. Amherst: University of Massachusetts, 7.

Hamilton, W. 1997, July 7. "We're so Excited . . . ," Cartoon in *The New Yorker*, 31.

Hau, K. and F. Salili. 1996. " Achievement Goals and Causal Attributions of Chinese Students." In *Growing Up the Chinese Way: Chinese Child and Adolescent Development*, edited by S. Lau. Hong Kong: Chinese University Press, 121–145.

Hertsgaard, M. 1997, November. "Our Real China Problem." *The Atlantic Monthly*, 97–114.

Hong, M. (Ed.). 1993. *Growing Up Asian American*. New York: Avon Books.

Hong, T. 1997, June/July. "Beyond Biology." *A. Magazine: Inside Asian America*, 35–41.

Huang, B. H. 1998, Winter. "Building a Bridge." *Families with Children from China: Greater New York, Connecticut, New Jersey*. Vol. 5, no. 1, 1, 3.

Huang, L. H. 1976. "The Chinese American Family." In *Ethnic Families in America: Patterns and Variations*, edited by C. H. Mindel and R. W. Habenstein. New York: Elsevier North-Holland, Inc., 124–147.

International Concerns Committee for Children. 1992. *Report on Intercountry Adoption*.

Jaret, C. 1995. *Contemporary Racial and Ethnic Relations*. New York: HarperCollins College Publishers.

Johnson, K. 1998. "Adoption and Abandonment in China." *Population and Development Review*, 24(3): 469–512.

Kim, D. S. 1977. "How They Fared in American Homes: A Follow-up Study of Adopted Korean Children in the United States." *Children Today* (6): 2–6, 36.

LaFromboise, H. L., K. Coleman, and J. Gerton. 1993. "Psychological Impact of Biculturalism: Evidence and Theory." *Psychological Bulletin* 114(3): 395–412.

Lau, J. M. 1998, January. "To Save a Child." *Reader's Digest*, 96–101.

Lau, S. (Ed.). 1996. *Growing Up the Chinese Way: Chinese Child and Adolescent Development*. Hong Kong: Chinese University Press.

Lehr, D. 1996, October 8. "The Riddle of Julia Ming Gale." *Boston Globe*, Living Arts section E, E1+.

Lie, J. 1995. "From International Migration to Transnational Diaspora." *Contemporary Sociology* 24(4): 303–306.

Loisel, L. 1996, July 5. "Baby Girls from China." *Hampshire Life Magazine*, 8–13.

Lowe, P. 1993. "Father Cures a Presidential Fever." In *Growing Up Asian American*, edited by M. Hong. New York: Avon Books, 175–190.

Miller, H. C. 1971. "Recent Developments in Korean Services for Children." *Children*, 18: 28–30.

Mills, C. W. 1959. *The Sociological Imagination*. New York: Grove Press.

Ou, Y. S. and H. P. McAdoo. 1993. "Socialization of Chinese American Children." In *Ethnicity: Strength in Diversity*, edited by H. P. McAdoo. Newbury Park, CA: Sage, 245–270.

Peplau, L. A. and S. E. Taylor (Eds.). 1997. *Sociocultural Perspectives in Social Psychology*. Upper Saddle River, NJ: Prentice Hall.

Perea, J. F. 1997. "The Statue of Liberty: Notes from Behind the Gilded Door." In *Immigrants Out!*, edited by J. F. Perea. New York: New York University Press, 44–58.

Porter, B. 1993, April 11. "I Met My Daughter at the Wuhan Foundling Hospital." *New York Times Magazine*, 24+.

Portes, A. and M. Zhou. 1994. "Should Immigrants Assimilate?" *Public Interest* 116: 18–33.

Ramos, J. D. 1996. "Intercultural Adoption." In *Focal Point: A National Bulletin on Family Support & Children's Mental Health*. Portland, OR: Portland State University, 13–16.

Register, C. 1991. *Are Those Kids Yours? American Families with Children Adopted from Other Countries*. New York: Free Press.

Reist, M. T. 1995. "China's One-Child Policy." In *China for Women: Travel and Culture*, edited by Feminist Press. New York: Feminist Press, 98–104.

Riley, N. E. 1997. "American Adoptions of Chinese Girls: The Socio-Political Matrices of Individual Decisions." *Women's Studies International Forum* 20(1): 87–102.

Robertson, I. 1981. *Sociology*. 2nd ed. New York: Worth Publishers Inc.

Rotheram, M. J. and J. S. Phinney. 1987. "Introduction: Definitions and Perspectives in the Study of Children's Ethnic Socialization." In *Children's Ethnic Socialization: Pluralism and Development*, edited by J. S. Phinney and M. J. Rotheram. Newbury Park, CA: Sage, 10–31.

Schaefer, R. T. 1993. *Racial & Ethnic Groups*. 5th ed. New York: HarperCollins College Publishers.

Schaefer, R. T. 1995. *Race and Ethnicity in the United States*. New York: HarperCollins College Publishers.

Scott, J. 1997, August 19. "Orphan Girls of China at Home in New York." *New York Times*, Metro section A, p. 1 and section B, 4–5.

Silverman, A. R. 1993. "Outcomes of Transracial Adoption." *The Future of Children: Adoption* 3(1):104–118.

Simon, R. 1994. "Transracial Adoption: The American Experience." In *In the Best Interests of the Child: Culture, Identity and Transracial Adoption*, edited by I. Gaber and J. Aldridge. London: Free Association Books, 137–150.

Skeldon, R. 1996. "Migration from China." *Journal of International Affairs* 49(2): 435–445.

Smith, J. F. 1996. "Analyzing Ethical Conflict in the Transracial Adoption Debate: Three Conflicts Involving Community." *Hypatia* 11(2): 1–33.

Smith, L. 1995, April 14. "Foreign Adoptions can Mean Joy—or Pain." *Los Angeles Times*, section E, 9.

Smolowe, J. 1996, January 22. "Saving the Orphans." *Time Magazine*, 41.

Soled, Debra E. (Ed.). 1995. *China: A Nation in Transition*. Washington, DC: Congressional Quarterly.

Spence, J. and A. Chin. 1996. *The Chinese Century: A Photographic History of the Last Hundred Years*. New York: Random House.

Sumida, S. H. 1993. "Afterword." In *Growing Up Asian American*, edited by M. Hong. New York: Avon Books, 399–405.

Summerfield, J. 1979. *Fodor's People's Republic of China*. New York: David McKay Co.

Tate, T. 1990. "Trafficking in Children for Adoption." In *Betrayal: A Report on Violence Toward Children in Today's World*, edited by C. Moorehead. New York: Doubleday, 143–165.

Thornton, M. C., L. M. Chatters, R. J. Taylor, and W. R. Allen. 1990. "Sociodemographic and Environmental Correlates of Racial Socialization by Black Parents." *Child Development* 61: 401–409.

Thurston, A. F. 1996, April. "In a Chinese Orphanage." *The Atlantic Monthly*, 28–30, 38–41.

Tyler, P. E. 1996, January 21. "In China's Orphanages, A War of Perception." *New York Times*, section H, 31.

U.S. Bureau of the Census. 1993. Current Population Reports, "Population Projections of the United States by Age, Sex, Race, and Hispanic Origin: 1993 to 2050." Washington, DC: U.S. Government Printing Office.

Wang, L. 1997a, October 26. "Laowai Adopt Chinese Babies: Home Visits to American and Canadian Families Who Adopted Chinese Children (Part I)." *Anhui Broadcasting Guide*, 15.

Wang, L. 1997b, November 2. "Laowai Adopt Chinese Babies: Home Visits to American and Canadian Families Who Adopted Chinese Children (Part II)." *Anhui Broadcasting Guide*, 16.

Weil, R. H. 1984. "International Adoptions: The Quiet Migration." *International Migration Review* XVIII, 2: 276–293.

Wong, H. M. 1989. *Exploring the Yangtze: China's Longest River*. San Francisco, CA: China Books & Periodicals, Inc.

Yee, P. 1989. *Tales from Gold Mountain: Stories of the Chinese in the New World*. New York: Macmillan Publishing Company.

"Your Up-to-the-Minute Guide to Summer '97 in the Hamptons." 1997, August. *Vanity Fair*, 82.

Youtz, D. 1997, Fall. "American Parents, Chinese Children: A Sino-American Experience for the 1990s." *Yale-China Review* 5 (2): 5–11.

WORLD WIDE WEB PAGES

Adoption Quest. 1998. *What Is a Home Study?* Available via http://www.nac.adopt.org/adopt/homestdy.html, April 30.

Caughman, S. 1998. *FCC Chapters and Local Contacts.* Last modified 3/21/98. Available via http://www.fwcc.org/contacts.html, April 30.

Osborne, M. 1997. "Halt of Russian Adoption?" *RainbowKids.com: An Online International Adoption Publication.* Available via http://www.rainbowkids.com/index.1296.html, December 3.

Wilken, K. 1995. "Controlling Improper Financial Gain in International Adoptions." *Duke Journal of Gender, Law & Policy,* Available via http://www.law.duke.edu/journals/djglp/djgv2a5.htm, May 7.

NEWSLISTS

Organization of Chinese Americans. 1997. "APAs Meet with Pres. Clinton and VP Gore." Available via oca@ari.net, December 12.

INDEX

About the Authors

RICHARD TESSLER is Professor of Sociology and Associate Director of the University of Massachusetts's Social and Demographic Research Institute. Professor Tessler has published extensively on social welfare issues.

GAIL GAMACHE is Professor of Sociology at the University of Massachusetts, Amherst. Her research has been present in numerous academic and professional journals.

LIMING LIU is a Ph.D. candidate in Sociology at the University of Massachusetts, Amherst and a research assistant at the Social and Demographic Research Institute.